The Completely and Totally True Book of URBaN LegENds

by Ann Fiery

illustrated by Mark Ulriksen

RUNNING PRESS
PHILADELPHIA · LONDON

D1088802

To my best friend, favorite art director, and beautiful wife, Leslie.
—Mark

9 8 7 6 5 4 3 2 1
Digit on the right indicates the number of this printing

Library of Congress Cataloging-in-Publication Number
2001087056

ISBN 0-7624-1074-4

Cover and interior illustrations by Mark Ulriksen
Design by Frances J. Soo Ping Chow
Edited by Molly Jay and Caroline Tiger
Typography: Imperfect and Universe

This book may be ordered by mail from the publisher.
Please include $2.50 for postage and handling.
But try your bookstore first!

Running Press Book Publishers
125 South Twenty-second Street
Philadelphia, Pennsylvania 19103-4399

Visit us on the web!
www.runningpress.com

Contents

URban LEGenDs and the Persistence of the FAbulous

All of us have heard them. Most of us have repeated them. Some of us have believed in them. But none of us has actually played a part in them. They are urban legends, of course, that unstoppable phenomenon of American life. Recklessly reproduced on the Internet, in the newspapers and tabloids, on television, and out of our own mouths, they swarm across the country like so many killer bees (urban legend!), populating the American mind with visions of murder and mayhem, pollutants and punishments. Our kidneys are being stolen. Our fried chicken has dead rats in it. The mere flick of our headlights could result in death. Foreigners play vile tricks on us. It matters little that sober reflection and a vast array of research contradicts most of these tales, or, at least, documents their infrequency; that is not the point. Urban legends have a function far surpassing fact, and that is to express—in the outlandish manner of dreams—the anxieties of our culture.

And, believe me, we have a lot of anxieties: What's that in my food? What's that in my pipes? What's that underneath my bed? Am I being betrayed by someone who is supposed to love me? Will evil be punished? Are there things I haven't even thought of that will kill me? Are people what they seem? AM I SAFE?

No.

It may, however, be comforting to learn that this news is not new. Our fears are the not-very-distant descendents of the fears that permeated society in the nineteenth century, and the eighteenth, and the seventeenth. The literature of those fears—what we now call fairy tales—were the urban legends of their era. Like ours, those legends, featuring young/pure/pretty/noble/innocent/poor girls and children threatened with murder/rape/cannibalism/abandonment ask the question, AM I SAFE? And then, as now, the answer is no. Though their up-to-the-moment accessories include computers, microwaves, and cell-phones, urban legends betray truly ancient angst.

Where, you may ask doubtfully, are the fairies? In our modern tales, nobody gets transformed into a princess by a benevolent fairy godmother; they get their intestines broiled in a tanning salon. Hardly seems analogous, you might grumble. True enough. But to demand the sudden appearance of a fairy is to miss the significance of the fairy tale. The fairy herself is merely the righter of preexistent wrongs: Cinderella was beautiful, good, and small footed; the fairy just gave her the opportunity to go public. The point of the Cinderella story is that the wicked stepsisters are punished for their vanity and sloth and justice is served. Strangely enough, that is also the point of the tanning salon narrative. If a young woman is so vain that she goes to a tanning salon and so slothful that she falls asleep there, then she deserves to have her intestines broiled. Furthermore, the impulse to visit the tanning salon in the first place is deeply suspect, resulting, as it does, in a false, unnatural suntan. It is a lie, and, in the world of legend, lies must be punished. Presto! Broiled intestines!

Okay, you admit, perhaps fairies are expendable. But what about the living-happily-ever-after bit? Urban legends tend to wind up in a spasm of gore: heads are rolling down staircases, marriages are ruined, people are throwing up. True enough, but the reader of the legends lives happily ever after because he has been saved from making the fateful mistakes that would result in his head rolling down the staircase. Thus, the happy ending of fairy tales does exist in urban legends, through the increased understanding of the legend's audience. The object, it seems to me, of all these narratives, whether from the eighteenth century or the twenty-first, is prevention. If you know the worst, you can avoid it.

Take the case of Little Red Riding Hood. It is true that in many versions of the story, Red Riding Hood and her granny are liberated from the belly of the beast (although in some versions they stay digested). This is a reasonably happy ending, but no one could mistake it for the gist of the story, which is that Appearances Are Deceiving (or possibly that Travel Is Dangerous). Compare the Legend of the Turkish Dog (vacationing family brings home a nice little dog, which turns out to be a very large rat); once the family learns that their pet is actually a rat, they dispose of it and probably live happily ever after. But the message of the tale, the reason for telling it, is exactly that of Little Red Riding Hood: Appearances Are Deceiving and Travel Is Dangerous. Watch out! it says. What you think you're seeing is not what you're really seeing! In foreign countries, rats look like dogs! Ignorance will result in a terrible disease!

If urban legends are our fairy tales, then we must acknowledge that they have been given a shabby treatment. Derided and debunked, they straggle along on a few websites devoted to their eradication and survive through the time-honored method of oral tradition. How will future generations pass these tales on to their grandchildren if we do not record them now? Unimaginable as it seems, it is entirely possible that the Legend of the Microwaved Dog could disappear from the face of the earth unless immediate conservation measures are taken.

Library shelves groan under the weight of hundreds of volumes of fairy tales, beautifully illustrated by the leading artists of their era, while our precious cache of urban legends is deposited in a mere three or four books. Forget wolves and fairies, princes, dwarves, and sleeping beauties; urban legends are our stories. They record our millennial terrors, our belief in the triumph of the wronged, our delight in the destruction of the villain, and our secret hope that technology will be wiped off the face of the earth. Violent, improbable, and lurid as they are, urban legends are our legacy, and we have an obligation to look beneath their heaving surface to see the noble mythology that lies there.

To this end, we have compiled a treasury of our best urban legends—the most exciting, beloved, and morally loaded tales that have traveled across the airwaves, through the wires, and up and down the dormitory hallways of America. We have scrutinized hundreds of versions of each of the legends that appears herein, searching for the archetypal story that lay within each of the variants. We have compared regional renditions, traveled far and wide to find the best sources, and destroyed a slew of imposter legends. We have interviewed people who claimed to have seen the kitchen where the dog was microwaved (and one person who said she had done it); we have heard from the kidney-deprived, the rat-consuming, and the adultery-discovering. We have listened to amazing tales and amazingly boring tales. We have suffered. But it was worth it, because now we have the latest and the best in urban legends, the uncut gems of our literary heritage.

WaRm ^{as}Toast

Once upon a time, there was a wealthy but witless woman named
Eusebia French. As her husband had long ago died in what police
had declared an entirely accidental incident and as she had no children due to their
being noisy and dirty, she lived alone in a grand house with her little Pekingese dog,
Vince, who dined on grilled sirloin and consequently had gout. Eusebia French had
a maid, Marlene, and a gardener, Boyd, but whenever anyone asked, she said,
"Vince and I live for each other alone." She often mentioned how she ground up
Vince's sirloin with her own hands (actually, she used a food processor). That was
nearly all she did with her hands, except get them manicured every week at the So
Long Nail Shoppe (where she never left a tip, because, she said, "It spoils them")
and shuffle cards during her canasta game.

Well, after working together for twenty-three years, Marlene and Boyd
inevitably fell in love and decided to marry. When they requested simultaneous vacation time in order to indulge themselves in a honeymoon, Eusebia French fired them
on the spot. "The nerve!" huffed Eusebia French.

Unfortunately, their departure left Eusebia in something of a pickle, for Maids
Ahoy Domestic Services failed to provide her with suitable replacements. The first
gardener refused to use pesticide on the roses, and the maid took a coffee break.
The second batch was no better, and Eusebia was soon at her wit's end. Vince, too,
was nettled by the disturbance to his routine, which he expressed by peeing on the
rug. Eusebia dropped a towel on the puddle and waited for five minutes. Using tongs,
she carried the towel out to the garbage can and threw both the towel and tongs
away. They had been good tongs and the whole episode left her dismayed.

Eight days passed and Eusebia noticed something even more dismaying. She
was running out of food. After much reflection, she decided to go to the store. It took
her the better part of the morning to get dressed (many of her favorite outfits were
in the laundry basket), and then she was confronted with the problem of Vince, for

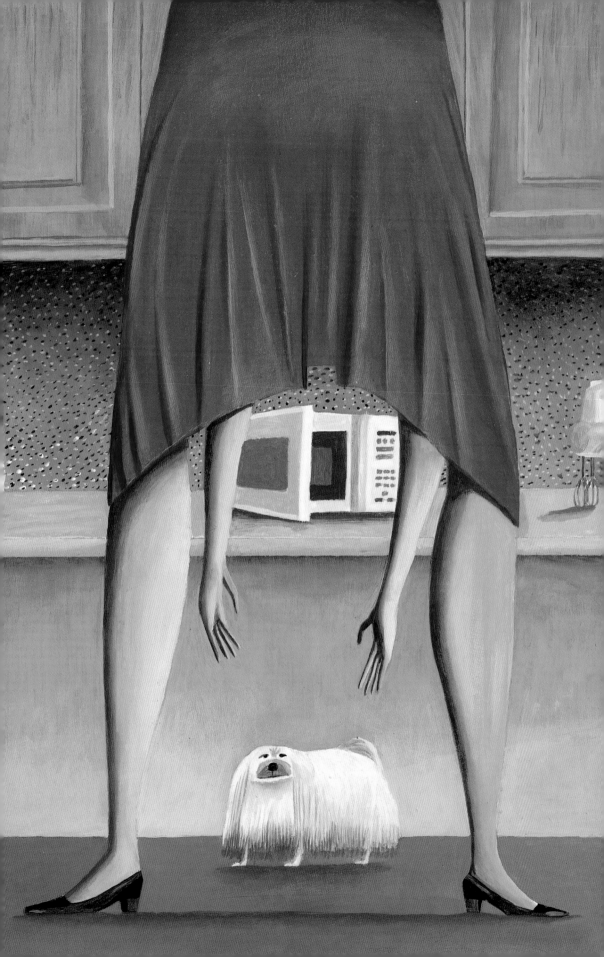

of course he must accompany her. But he was dirty. He even had a dustball on his stomach fur, which made Eusebia ache with the desire to reprimand Marlene, who had been in charge of keeping Vince and the house clean. Instead, she gritted her teeth and ran him a tub. In the spirit of the moment, she threw in some Tea Rose bath salts for extra beautification, and picked up the little dog.

"Come to sudsies, Vincey-vince," she cooed.

Vince howled and struggled. The ingratitude! Eusebia was furious. Her own bath salts! "And they aren't cheap, Vince!" she cried. She held on to him firmly and dropped his back end into the water.

"Aaa-oooow," said Vince.

"Shut up!" said Eusebia. She clutched him more firmly still and began to scrub.

Vince struggled and barked and clawed, until, in the end, he ripped a hole in Eusebia's hard-won blouse. Eusebia was enraged. She yanked the dog from the tub, screaming "Aaa! Aaa! Aaa! My blouse! Now I have to change my clothes! You nasty little shit!" She stalked off to the closet, where she found an old pink wool skirt and a silk blouse she had forgotten about. Accessorizing was in order, and it was half an hour before Eusebia remembered Vince.

When she ran back to the bathroom, she found him shivering piteously on the cold floor. He was drenched and miserable, and his gouty paw lay uselessly on the tile. Eusebia French felt a wave of remorse—her first—as she knelt near the dog.

"Vincey, my precious little moo-moo. Mommy's so sorry!"

"Wee," replied Vince.

Eusebia was faced with a dilemma: wrap Vince in one of her own fleecy pink towels? With no foreseeable means of laundering it? She reflected on her love for Vince. But he was, after all, a dog. And he was looking rather repulsive right now.

"Wee," sighed Vince.

A call to action. Suddenly, Eusebia French was blessed with an inspiration. She picked up the dripping dog and, and holding him as far away from her blouse as she could, she went downstairs. Her first thought had been to put him in the dryer, but when she entered the kitchen, her eyes fell on the microwave oven. How much more efficient! Vince would be warm and dry in no time!

Eusebia French stuffed Vince onto the revolving plate inside the oven. "Wee," whimpered Vince. She pondered the correct amount of time for a wet dog, and finally concluded that as he could take no longer than a potato; four minutes seemed suitable.

"Warm as toast in just a wink," said Eusebia French as she closed the door with a snap and pressed the start button.

BRonZe
gOddeSS

In July, wheat shimmered like a sea of gold with each tiny gust of air. The air was thick with heat and the dusty richness of ripe corn. A faint, pungent scent of blackberry lay beneath the strong crop smells, and in the earliest part of the morning, when the sky was still gray and the sun had not begun to bake the air and the land and the town into some sort of clay version of themselves, the blackberry smell ran like cool water along the edges of the yards and down into the dried creeks. Raccoons would stop their acrobatic battles with garbage cans and sniff a little, surprised, at the winey aroma.

At that hour, Imogene was still asleep. Imogene did not get up until 8:10. By that time the blackberry scent was long gone, but even if it hadn't been, Imogene wouldn't have smelled it. Imogene had no use for blackberry scent; what Imogene wanted was Travesty, the new urban fragrance from Adorno, in a purse-sized atomizer. She would have settled for Upstart, the heady scent of the new millenium, also in a purse-sized atomizer, but she really wanted Travesty.

At 8:20 Imogene was in the kitchen. She was wearing a bright green sweatshirt. It said Born to Shop on the front in big pink letters, but Imogene couldn't think about that now because she was late to work. She was frantically stirring her NutriSlim and blowing on some fingernail polish she had just applied to a hole in her stockings. Her mother, Marth, impassive, sat at the dinette reading a magazine.

"It says here that Cindy Crawford and Leonardo DiCaprio went to the DanceAid banquet together."

Imogene stopped stirring. "No. She's way too old for him."

"I'm just telling you what it says."

"No way. Let me see."

Her mother threw the magazine at her.

"Oh, you can tell they faked the picture. Totally." Imogene resumed her stirring. "What—Look, here's a good one: 'What's Your Man-Pleasing Potential?' It's a quiz."

"Ask me one."

"I prefer lacy, sexy lingerie to plain white underwear. Agree. Agree somewhat. Disagree." Imogene looked at Marth questioningly.

"Agree."

"Well, duh. This is stupid. You know what I want? I want one of those body slimmer things. See? It's only $32.95."

"I thought you already got one?"

"I got the Svelte Shape. It's different."

"Doesn't it do the same thing?"

"No. The body slimmer thing is for your thighs. Oh look, here are those Nite Lite shoes. Very nice."

"What's the matter with your thighs?"

"Oh Mom, they're huge. Gross. I can't even wear my bike shorts anymore."

"You wore them on Saturday."

"Yeah, but that's because I couldn't think of anything else. Do these look okay?" She pulled up her stockings. The dot of pink polish strained, but held.

"Fine," said Marth without looking.

Imogene disappeared down the carpeted hallway toward her bedroom. The walls were lined with Imogene—at two, her hands clasped against her rosebud cheek in a photographer's coy pose; at eight, school picture, scrawny in a bright flowered dress, missing many teeth; at eleven, still scrawny, lank hair combed flat against her head, eyes anxious; at thirteen, no longer scrawny in a tight blue t-shirt, black mascara freckling the skin beneath her eyes; and the graduation portrait of Imogene's head floating on a sea of pink feathers (she had chosen the boa option; the drape option was for geeks), her hair defying gravity in elaborate spangled clips and her eyes heavy with glittering eyeshadow. Interspersed with the photographs of Imogene were two large color portraits of a German shepherd and one of a horse. "Beauty, 1977–1997" read a plaque underneath the picture of the horse.

"Okay, how's this? Oh God, I'm late," Imogene stood in front of her mother.

"It looks good," Marth said, surveying her critically. "I like the purple with the aqua."

"Which shoes?" Imogene produced a pair of black, precariously high heels and a pair of frosted pink pumps with tiny Mylar rosettes at the toe.

"Oh, the black definitely. The pink doesn't go at all."

"Good. Thanks. You know that purse that Cinda had yesterday?"

"No. I guess I didn't see it."

"Little? Sort of a rectangle? It was really cute—and practical. I really need something like that. I was thinking of going to Falconmooe on lunch."

"Did it have all those zippers? I don't like the ones with all the zippers."

"No, it's just sort of small, with a little change purse on the front. Hers was taupe, but she said it comes in green and red and black and slate. I thought I'd get the slate. God, I'm so late. Harvey's going to kill me!"

"Wait and go after work. I could meet you."

"Oh, that'd be great—wait, no. I can't. I've got an appointment at TonRika's."

"What time?" asked Marth.

"The only time she could get me in was 5:15. I'm going to have to leave work early. There. Is that too much blusher?" Imogene turned around

"No, it's good. What is it?"

"Mmmm," said Imogene, squinting at the little compact, "Burnt raisin."

"Well, when are you going to be through at TonRika's? We could go to Falconmooe after."

"I could meet you at like 6:30."

"That's good with me. I've got a little shopping to do anyway. I've got to get some polish remover and I want one of those basketball games—you know, the hoop things—for Joey."

"You can get them much cheaper at Wal-Mart."

"It's not that much cheaper."

"Than Tencer's? Way cheaper."

"Well. So let's meet at Love Burger at what—6:45?" said Marth, changing the subject.

"Okay." Imogene was distracted, searching through her purse. "Oh. Here it is." She pulled out a crushed tube of suntan lotion. "I need some more of this stuff. God, gotta go, gotta go." She pulled a large plastic shopping bag into the crook of her arm and on her shoulder she arranged her purse, which bulged with an assortment of items. She carried a shoebox in her other hand and tucked a thermos of NutriSlim under her arm. She put her car keys in her teeth and walked out the front door.

Imogene reached American Home Financial by 9:40. Harvey was waiting impatiently near her cubicle, kicking his shoe against its metal rim and hitching up his belt, so she settled right down to work, efficiently clicking her pink fingernails against the keys of the adding machine, writing numbers in her precise handwriting in minuscule spaces on forms, and writing letters that began, "Unfortunately, we are unable to provide the requested statement(s), as there has not been any activity on your account for more than thirty days. A deposit or an interest deposit will not activate your account once it has become inactive. We apologize for any inconvenience this may cause. We thank you for the opportunity to serve your financial needs. Sincerely, Item Processing, American Home Financial." It was a day like every other day. Imogene mixed two cuplets of nondairy creamer into her coffee. Imogene stopped to say hi to Kelly and see if she had found shoes to go with her wedding dress yet. When Stacy brought her baby in, Imogene said, "Oh, he's such a cutie!" Imogene poured out her NutriSlim. Imogene carefully outlined her lips in the bathroom. Imogene and Harvey agreed that Saturday night TV used to be better. "I love that color on you," said Imogene about Dayna's blouse.

Finally it was 5:00. "I have an appointment, Harvey," said Imogene. "I took a short lunch," she added helpfully.

By 5:15, she was in the parking lot. TonRika's Tanning was off to one side of a tiny mall, just a boring mall with a Chinese restaurant, a One-Stop Mailing Center, and the Red Rose Nail Salon.

TonRika, exotically swathed in a gold and black turban, greeted Imogene as she walked through the door. "Honey! Imogene!" She swayed dramatically on her stool, inspecting Imogene's face. "It's the middle of July, but you've got that winter white look! Definitely time for a treatment!" She leaned close to Imogene, exuding bourbon, "I would say you could use some products, babe."

"Like what?" said Imogene with interest.

"I see you with kind of an all-over bronze look. Like Chine, you know?"

"What's Chine?"

"You know, the supermodel."

"Oh. Oh yeah. I didn't know how you said it."

"Chin-ay. But see, look in this picture," TonRika trotted over to a small formica end table laden with magazines. She waved one at Imogene. "Don't you think?"

"Look at that bathing suit. I love it."

TonRika squinted at the picture. "It's great," she said carelessly, "but look at that tan! Bronze. Totally bronze."

"Do you think it'd look good on me?" asked Imogene.

"Look at your features," TonRika crowed, emitting a cloud of bourbon. "You are like a total bronze goddess!"

"I am?" said Imogene earnestly, trying to catch a glimpse of herself in the mirror.

"Totally. But for that you have to use this Sun Systems Bronzing Créme. See," said TonRika, producing several tubes and bottles, "first you have to exfoliate with Sun Systems Refreshing Rinse. It's made from all natural products. Then you hydrate with Sun Systems Emollient Elixer. Smell. They put sage in it. Totally natural. Then you can use the Bronzing Créme, because your skin has been, like, stripped of all the toxins. So it goes in."

"Gee," said Imogene, "How much does it cost."

"Forty-four ninety-five for everything, which is pretty good, considering."

"And this is enough for a couple times, right?"

"Oh sure. Three, at least. So it's only fifteen dollars per treatment."

"That's cheap," said Imogene, getting out her wallet. "Oh, I guess I'm maxed on my Visa. I'll do a check."

"That's fine," said TonRika.

So Imogene repaired to the dressing room and exfoliated and emolliated. Then she rubbed Bronzing Créme on every iota of her flesh. She stuck her head out the dressing room door. "I'm ready."

TonRika hastily emerged from under the counter. "Just checking something," she announced unsteadily. "Okay, honey, go on into the Malibu Room. Actually, you can go into the Tahiti Room if you want. My 5:00 cancelled." She straightened her turban.

"Okay," said Imogene, waving.

She settled herself on the table, put the pillow patches over her eyes, and closed the lid above her. Out in the lobby, TonRika switched the lamps on. Imogene loved this part, slowly growing warmer and warmer, beginning to feel minute droplets of sweat coat her arms and chest. She stretched for a moment, her muscles and bones straining and then relaxing again. It was so nice and warm. She pointed her toes, luxuriating in her body. So nice and warm. For a minute, she could feel every piece of herself—fingers, arms, elbows, neck, chin, ears, hair, everything—and she felt rich and satisfied. Then she fell asleep.

TonRika decided that sitting on a stool was what was ruining her back. "I got to get a chair. I got to get one of those ergonomic chairs," she mumbled, rubbing her spine. She took her glass over to the waiting area and cleared a space for it on the small formica table. Then she stretched herself out on the sofa. She was in the middle of a good article—it was on the former hairstyles of the stars—when she, too, fell asleep.

At 7:15, Marth decided she'd just go ahead and eat. She got the diet cheeseburger and a salad and a diet soda. She didn't like eating alone. After dinner, she did a little more shopping. She wanted some of that Burnt Raisin blusher.

At 8:15, TonRika awoke.

She straightened her turban and assumed the indignant expression of one unrightfully accused of sleep, but there was no one there to accuse her. So she puttered around, removing all traces of her long nap, plumping pillows, reclustering bottles, daintily rinsing her bourbon glass. When the thought of Imogene finally popped into her head, TonRika gasped with fury. The girl had tiptoed out without paying! "You try to be nice and do someone a favor, like the Tahiti Room, and what do you get? Heartache!" TonRika stormed towards the dressing room, sure that Imogene had left a pile of greasy towels on the floor. But there was nothing, except Imogene's purple and aqua dress hanging limply from a hanger.

TonRika stared at the hanger for a long time. Seemingly of its own accord, her hand reached up to straighten her turban. Finally, she took a deep breath and walked resolutely to the Tahiti Room. She could tell what had happened as soon as she opened the door—it was the smell. With more fortitude than could be reasonably expected of her, TonRika reached to the controls on the side of the tanning bed and turned off the lamps. But she could go no farther, so it was, ultimately, Hugh Ortiz, the ambulance driver, who first glimpsed what Imogene had become. "Shriveled," he said solemnly into the news camera, "and sort of, sort of—brown. Brownish purple. It was like she had been dried out. Exploded, and then dried out. She looked strange."

such Clean FlooRs

Once upon a time there was an exceedingly unfortunate little town called Millard. By some fluke of geography, Millard was subject to hurricanes and blizzards, not at the same time, of course, but still. A rare pollen, previously known only in Zaire, came to Millard in the spring of 1992 and gave all the cows asthma. Most of the cows died, horribly. The town's leading industry—tennis-related outerwear—had been on the decline since the late seventies and finally gave up the ghost in 1993, causing mass unemployment and a surging crime rate. The Millard sports teams never won a tournament, Millard children were always last in the state debating championships, and Millard girls never became beauty queens.

However, the townspeople of Millard continued to laugh and love, get born, get married, and die peacefully. Certainly they complained about the weather and bemoaned the unemployment rate. But they cheered for the football team and took the children out for ice cream after each debating fiasco. The people over in the next town, Coffee, said with grudging admiration, "They ain't got much in Millard, except spunk."

But then disaster struck. At first, it didn't seem any worse than anything else that had happened in Millard: food poisoning. Every single solitary chicken delivered by Frenchy's Fresh Vacuum-Pak Poultry on the week of May 27 was riddled with salmonella bacteria (the vacuum-packaging system "sort of broke," according to Buck "Frenchy" Bontemps). Sad to say, all those chickens were destined for consumption at the Millard Memorial Day Picnic. Since it had been snowed out the previous year, the picnic was exceptionally well attended this time, despite an ominous stillness in the air and lowering black clouds in the east. All Millardians partook lustily of the tasty fried chicken.

Well, it was right in the middle of the softball game that the effects began to be felt. Some players doubled over in the field and some ran for the dugout. In the bleachers, whole families began to race for the restrooms together. More privacy-conscious folk

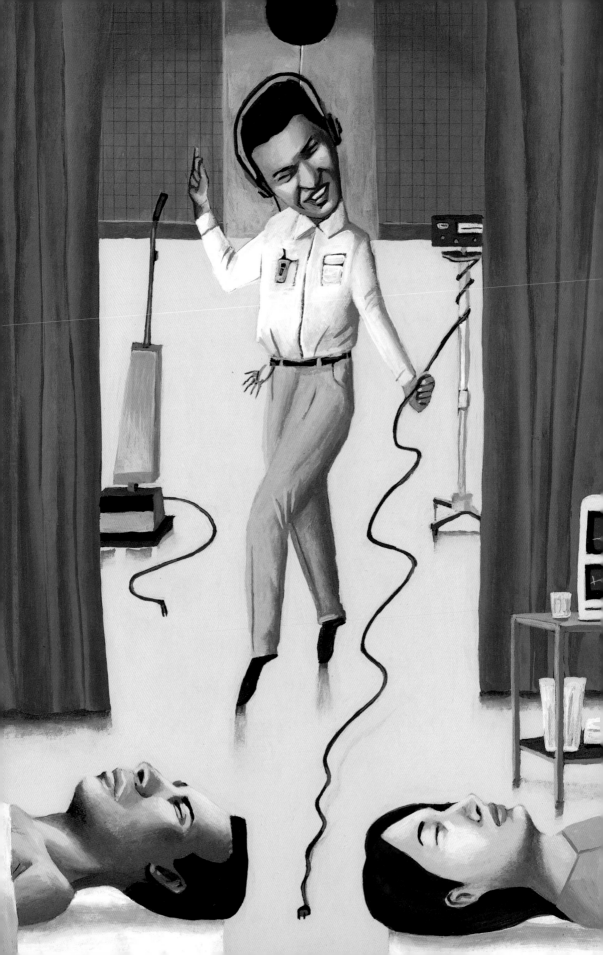

bolted for their cars. Then the brewing storm broke; rain poured from the black and yellow clouds in sheets. Tree branches lashed back and forth in a sudden eruption of wind. And think: Where is the cream of Millard? Crouched in the dugout, prone in the outfield, gasping in the restrooms, or desperately trying to drive their cars. The lightning commenced with a crash and did not cease for an hour. The outfielders took the brunt of it, but the dugout was struck repeatedly, until the ground was littered with the bodies of the injured. The restroom dwellers fared better; only those who were actually touching the stall doors were felled. As for the cars, it was a toss-up—wise Millardians who stayed in their cars were saved, but foolish Millardians who pulled over to vomit were smited. Millard's ditches were soon full of paralyzed picnickers.

Amidst this sea of tragedy, one Millardian rejoiced. Dr. Halbert House, the young and vigorous doctor at Coffee General Hospital, had a spanking new Intensive Care Unit, chockablock with gleaming heart monitors, life-support machines, electroencephalograms, and ventilators. The only thing it lacked was patients. Six scrupulously clean, fully equipped rooms sat waiting for the deathly ill to come and lie down in them. Now, thought Dr. House, wriggling gleefully inside his spotless white coat, eighty-six opportunities to test my equipment.

As they brought the first batch in, Dr. House was in his element, directing this stretcher to that room, that stretcher to this room. The hospital's halls were soon lined with the overflow, but Dr. House's attention was focused on the twelve patients occupying his ICU beds and, more importantly, hooked up to his machines. What an extravaganza of medical competence: oxygen bubbled through tubes, nurses raced behind IVs and bags of blood, EEGs crackled authoritatively, X-rays buzzed, heart monitors beeped softly, ventilators wheezed gently, and Dr. House stood in the middle, his eyes glowing with triumph.

By midnight, he felt as if he at least deserved a medal. Resting his feet on top of his desk in his little office, Dr. House contemplated the twelve occupants of his ICU with pride. There they were, lives saved, sleeping soundly—all due to his efforts. When Dr. House finally went home, he slept the sleep of the righteous.

However, when he returned to the hospital at ten the next morning, he was told that both patients in Room Four had up and died. Dr. House was furious. He yelled at the nurses. He screamed at the resident. He stormed over to Room Four to see for himself. Yes, they were certainly dead, but why? Dr. House considered. He looked at their charts. He looked at their graphs and scans. It all seemed reasonably straightforward. Both patients had been progressing normally until—Boom!—they died of heart failure at 6:02 a.m.

"Goddammit!" yelled Dr. House at the two corpses. His only comfort was that he had plenty of replacements. The seventy-four lightning-struck Millardians who did not fit in Dr. House's ICU had been farmed out to other units, so he picked a pair of forty-year-old, lightning-struck twins who were languishing in Dermatology and popped them into Room Four. Resolving not to cry over spilt milk, Dr. House continued his inspection of the remaining ten patients. They were advancing precisely on schedule. Dr. House patted his new machines lovingly. He envisioned the becoming look of modest satisfaction that would appear on his face as he walked toward the governor to receive his medal of commendation. I need to develop a more dignified posture, he thought.

But the next morning, Dr. House was greeted with the news that the twins of Room Four had expired in the night. Or, rather, at 6:08 that morning. "I'll fire your ass!" screamed Dr. House to the nurse who delivered him the news. But try as he might, he could find no explanation for the demise of the stricken twins.

Feeling slightly queasy, Dr. House selected two more lightning victims for Room Four. These are both quite stable cases, he reassured himself. By tomorrow they'll be walking around complaining about the food.

On the contrary, the next morning they were dead.

After he ripped out a large hunk of his own hair, Dr. House went to Room Four for another look. There they were: the heart monitor, the IVs, the life-support system, the ventilator, the EEG, the oxygen pump, all these fresh accoutrements of lifesaving, all humming serenely over the two lifeless bodies.

Dr. House thought for several minutes before he left the room. And that afternoon, before the next two lightning-strike victims were rolled into the waiting beds of Room Four, two workmen, looking distinctly germy in the sterilized premises of the ICU, installed two surveillance cameras in the room.

Inside his office, Dr. House drank a pot of coffee and kept his eyes on the monitor all night long. At 4 a.m., one of the patients sneezed (which, by the way, was a sign of improvement). Other than that, absolutely nothing happened. The patients lay there like two loaves of bread, breathing evenly. By 5:45, Dr. House was holding his eyelids open with his fingers.

Suddenly, a torrent of humming exploded over the monitor. Dr. House's eyes jerked open, and he watched a man in headphones enter Room Four. It was Fabrizio, one of the hospital janitors, and he was clearly in the middle of a dance routine. "STOP! In the name of love," he mouthed, his eyes closed, his hips swinging from side to side, hand outstretched. He held the door open with one foot, and Dr. House could see that his floor polisher was in the hall outside the room. ". . . before you break my heart," Fabrizio whispered as he stooped down to the electrical outlet and pulled out all of the plugs with a deft flick of his wrist. "Think it o-over," he mouthed, snapping the plug of the floor polisher into the outlet and disappearing through the door. There was a moment of quiet as the life-support system went down, and then a soothing buzz as the polisher started up.

Snug as a bug

"**Don't know** what you want to go off for," grumbled Henry Farmer softly. He didn't exactly want Katie to hear him, but he also didn't want to be the kind of man who sat by with his hands folded while his one and only daughter threw herself in harm's way on account of some damn notion she had picked up on the television. "Should have thrown the damn thing out the day you were born," he whispered seditiously, zapping off the power.

"Turn it back on, Pop. My show's about to start."

Henry Farmer obediently turned on the television and watched several blonde-haired beauties telescope their long limbs into minute sports cars and race demonically through what were supposed to be the streets of Oslo. "60th Parallel" announced the titles in dashing script. Katie came in and flopped on the sofa, her eyes focused blinklessly on the screen before her. "See," she said, almost to herself, "Astrid's going to tell him she's in love with him and then she's going to arrest him. See?"

"Humph."

"Look, Pop, see how pretty it is? See those things there? Those are cafés, where everyone gathers in the evenings to listen to jazz."

Henry could tell that was quoted directly from that travel book, which, he had noted with suspicion, was called Scandinavia: Warm Heart of the Icy North.

"And they stay up all night in the summer because the sun doesn't set until, like, three. Oh, look, see, tears are sort of welling up in his eyes. He's really a romantic. Norwegians are really romantic, even though they seem so sporty with all those skis."

"They drink a lot, is all I know."

"Pop!" she said, finally losing patience. "I'm going and that's that. I've never been anywhere except Chicago that once, and I want to have the European experience of a lifetime. Don't you want me to be well educated and cosmopolitan? Don't you want me to see new sights and expand my horizons? Don't you realize that we have a global economy and we need to develop a global perspective?"

Henry wondered where she'd picked all this up. He opened his mouth to argue with her, and then noticed his wife, Marilyn, who was standing in the doorway waggling her eyebrows at him in a concentrated manner. This was a sign of thirty years duration. It meant "Shut up." So he did.

Katie departed on Thursday for her Scandinavian adventure, and an ominous silence followed. Finally, after two weeks, Henry and Marilyn received a postcard. The picture on the front was quite alarming: it was a painting of a skinny, bald fellow holding a hand over each ear. There was no telling what it meant, so Henry and Marilyn turned the card over.

Dear Mom and Dad,
*   This has been the most exciting week of my life. I'm hanging out with some*
super people I met at Akershus. Of course, we went to see the Munch museum
even though everyone says he's overrated.
*   Love, Katherine*

And that was all, for three more weeks. "I'm going to deck that child," Henry muttered as he switched on the milking machines.

But he didn't. When he saw Katie emerge from the airplane, he felt his jaw grow slack. Marilyn, beside him, let out an involuntary "Hun-uh!" Their Katie, who had embarked on her trip wearing a sensible and tidy pink sweatsuit, returned from it wearing a black micro-mini, a pair of high-heeled chartreuse boots, and an enormous purple sweater. Her hair, which had formerly been long and brown, was now short and red, and her thin lips were slippery under a coating of shiny brown lipstick.

They stared. She walked with prim, self-conscious steps toward them. "Hi, parents," she said casually, as though she'd been away for the weekend. They followed her careful steps toward the baggage claim, where one small bag awaited her.

"Didn't you buy any souvenirs?" cried Marilyn.

"Souvenirs? No, Mom, I didn't buy any *souvenirs*. I bought some clothes and I got a few really outstanding things that I sent back separately. Norwegian textile design is really cutting edge, you know," she said haughtily.

She warmed up once they got in the car (out of the public eye, thought Henry) and began to chatter about her trip. She talked on and on, needing no questions, nor even any sign of interest, to spur her on. For fifty miles, the words spilled forth: "In Europe, they . . . a European look . . . so sophisticated . . . a glass of wine with dinner . . . in this little cafe . . . women seem so much more chic . . . they shop for vegetables with these string bags . . . you can't believe how . . . then the music . . . we stayed up . . . "

And so it went. Norway, it appeared, was paradise on earth, and Katie did not tire of singing its praises. The United States, on the other hand, filled her with disdain. The landscape, the people, the food, the stores, and the coffee—all were mere vessels for her scorn. Henry hoped fervently that the song of Norway would fade and Katie would return to her old self, but, instead, she seemed to become more like her new self with each passing day. The arrival of her purchases brought on an especially intense spasm of Norwegian fervor. Katie kneeled by the box and reverently lifted the items from their packaging material. First came a wooden vase, which seemed like a nonsensical concept to Henry. "So simple," sighed Katie joyously. Then two mounted black-and-white photographs of triangles. "So graphic. So powerful." Then a pair of black shoes shaped like bricks. "So chic." And, finally, with a rapt, ecstatic face, Katie produced a large plastic-wrapped square of aqua and black. Henry and Marilyn looked at it quizzically. Expecting coos of admiration, Katie looked up at her parents when it failed to materialize. Their expressions seemed to enrage her.

"It's a duvet," she said resentfully.

"Oh," said Henry.

They looked at it for a few moments.

"What's a duvet?" asked Henry

"Oh, Father," said Katie with exaggerated patience. "It's like a comforter. That's what they call them there. They're filled with goose feathers instead of disgusting polyester fill. They're total-ly light, yet they keep you completely warm. Ths one is an Anderskand."

"What's an Anderskand?" asked Marilyn.

"God, Mother! Haven't you been listening to a word I've been telling you? Anderskand, Anderskand—it's the most famous duvet maker in Europe. These goose feathers are hand-plucked by this 500-year-old guild of goose-pluckers in Folda. They're famous for how fast they pluck them. Five minutes after they're dead, they're plucked." She fingered the plastic admiringly.

Henry couldn't help himself. "They sure cook your goose in Folda," he chortled.

Katie gave him a withering look.

"Maybe when you take it out of the wrapper, we'll see," said Marilyn soothingly.

"What, and put it next to my beautiful pink rosebud wallpaper? I think I'll just wait till I have a place of my own, if you know what I mean, Mom." Words cannot describe the bitterness with which she spoke.

"And not a minute too soon," said Henry, surprising himself and the others. Katie gathered up her goods and swept from the room, the picture of wounded dignity.

The duvet stayed packed in its plastic wrapper for four months, when Katie finally did find an apartment. It came attached to her new boyfriend, Gerhard, who, alas, wasn't Norwegian but did his best to overcome this setback with a laboriously acquired European flair. This involved much staying up late and dallying in cafés as well as carrying a sketchbook filled with reasonably good drawings. Katie thought he was wonderful, and, as this coincided with her discovery that her parents were dolts, she was eager to move in with him when he asked her.

Henry and Marilyn looked askance at the entire proceeding, but, as Katie informed them, she was twenty-two and could do whatever she damn well pleased. They suspected that her departure would be a relief.

It was. Katie loaded some clothes, her vase, her triangle photographs, her new black shoes, and her duvet into the truck, and she and Gerhard drove away. Henry and Marilyn watched her go, and when the truck finally disappeared at the end of the driveway, they both felt as though they had finished the last day of school before summer vacation. Henry whistled on the way to the barn.

Katie whistled, too, in her new apartment. She positioned her vase on top of Gerhard's CD player and hung her triangles up over the dinette. The effect, while not exactly Norwegian, was interesting. In the bedroom, she shoved aside Gerhard's running shoes and lined up her black shoes and chartreuse boots. She folded her sweaters and put them away in the drawers.

And then it was time to unveil the duvet. The plastic wrapping was much harder to get off than she had thought it would be, and the whole thing was really heavy, but when she straightened it over the bed and contemplated the bold aqua and black squiggles, she felt the first stirrings of domestic contentment. It was just so her. "Cool," she said.

"Hey. Cool," said Gerhard when he saw it.

Later that night, when they went to bed, Katie felt that same surge of satisfaction as she pulled up the duvet. Cool, she thought. It was heavier than she remembered, but cozy. She snuggled next to Gerhard and fell instantly to sleep.

Much later, she woke up. It was the thickest part of the night, and in the dark, unfamiliar room, she couldn't make out the walls or the door. The apartment house was completely silent.

Something was wrong.

What was it?

There's no noise, she thought. It can't be a burglar. She realized that she was dripping with sweat. I'm hot, she thought. My problem is that I'm hot.

Then the duvet moved.

At first she thought it was Gerhard, but he was motionless beside her. Then it moved again, the thick cotton heaving slightly against her skin. She noticed a shuddering against her shins. It felt sort of like having a cat walk over the bedspread when you're in bed. But Gerhard didn't have a cat.

"Gerhard!" she screamed.

"What!" he yelped, jerking awake.

"The duvet's moving!"

"Jesus, you scared me." He sat up groggily and turned the light on. "Gee, I'm hot."

"Gerhard, look—" she pointed. "It's moving."

"Moving?" he said, "what do you mean? It's not mo—oh my God, it's moving!"

And indeed, the duvet was heaving and writhing rhythmically, the puffy exterior surging up and down against their bodies.

"Aggggh!" screamed Gerhard, leaping out of bed.

Katie couldn't scream; she could only sit frozen, watching.

"Get out! Get out!" shouted Gerhard, but she didn't move.

Then, slowly, she got out of the bed and reached down to the side of the duvet cover, to the little plaque of buttons that covered the opening in the cover. She unbuttoned all the buttons and, swallowing hard, looked inside the duvet cover.

What Katie saw was a twining, slithering pinky-white mass. From the plucked tip of every goose-feather, a cluster of maggots had formed, and now hundreds of thousands of tiny worms lurched towards her. As the first several hundred spilled out of the duvet onto the floor, she began to run for home.

Something
borrowed

O**nce upon a time** there was a man named Standish Lewall, and he had a good thing going. Half of it was named Shirley and half of it was named MaryAnn, but you need to know about Standish before I can tell you what happened.

Sometimes in the morning, Standish would look at himself in the bathroom mirror and laugh. He'd say, "Standish, you are something else. You are a rare breed, baby."

And whoever it was in the next room would say, "Are you saying something, Standish? I can't hear you."

Standish would stop laughing and start to look how he appeared to the outside world, which was very, very beautiful. When he wasn't laughing, Standish looked like an amazed angel. He had high cheekbones and pale skin and round gray eyes and small white teeth. His clothes looked as though someone with exquisite taste had brought them to Standish's house and hung them gently in his closet on silky hangers, because Standish himself appeared far too unearthly to engage in anything so crass as shopping. Similarly, it was a shock to see Standish driving—though he did it gracefully—because the car was so metallic and mechanical, so unlike Standish.

Standish was not only beautiful, he was winning. "No!" he would protest, his round eyes widening in disbelief as he leaned across the table toward his date, who had just uttered some nondescript irony. And a surge of protectiveness would rip through the atmosphere like a cleaver. If the woman didn't reach out to stroke him right then and there, she certainly did later, when he unleashed his masterpiece: at the end of a bit of witty banter (he was good at that, too), Standish would suddenly—touchingly—blurt, "God! I love women!"

That usually took care of everything. When they woke up the next morning, Standish (very kindly, in his estimation) gave the woman a cup of coffee and sent her on her way. If she seemed to be missing the point or dallying too long in bed or, in one horrid instance, actually borrowing his bathrobe, he was more blunt. "Time to go, Loreen—no, sorry, Dana. I'll give you a call." On sundry occasions when this, too, failed to roust them, he would say something I can't even repeat.

Most of the women who met him were so unnerved to learn that he wasn't gay that they didn't ask questions. And most of them weren't around long enough to find out that he never had a girlfriend, that, in fact, he didn't have any friends at all. Every once in awhile, a woman would begin to confess to a friend about a humiliating experience she had had with a guy named Standish and the friend would clap her hand to her head and say, "Oh God, not Standish—that was the most embarrassing morning of my life. I thought he was so pure like an angel and that I was going to be"—and the first woman would interrupt and say, bitterly, "his first lover," and the other one would nod and they would compare notes on finding out just how far removed they were from his first lover and on being kicked out of bed, and then they would vow to hate him forever.

Meanwhile, Standish wasn't always laughing when he looked in the mirror. Sometimes it was a troublesome business, because he would note a new wrinkle, or worse, a new vertical wrinkle. Now, age on a man is a better deal than age on a woman, but age on a beautiful man is more wearing than you might think. A thin-haired angel is no angel at all. Which is why, when Standish Lewall met Shirley Simon, he altered his manner of doing business.

Shirley Simon was tall and robust, with rosy cheeks and heavy hair. She walked with a thumping tread through the hallways of power, swinging her briefcase and checking her watch because the day was simply too short for all the work she had to do. She was a woman with unquenchable energy and a ferocious ability to make profitable investments for her company, Monroe, Mercator & Orfing. She worked day and night and Sundays. She worked on President's Day. She worked on Labor Day. The only reason she didn't work on the 4th of July was that it was her brother's birthday. Monroe, Mercator & Orfing loved her. They shuddered to think where they would be without her. They paid her an astronomical salary only slightly smaller than their own. They gave her stock options and commissions and bonuses. She was rich, rich, rich.

Perfect, thought Standish, eyeing her thoughtfully. Plenty of money and plenty of business trips. Standish, baby, you will be a Man of Leisure. He took a quick look in a nearby mirror and floated toward the table where Shirley stood, eating celery and chatting with her best friend, MaryAnn DeBonventura.

A word about MaryAnn DeBonventura. She was as beautiful as Standish, and twice as worried about getting old. She, too, was notable for her method of dumping people, which involved a dramatic post-coital recitation, confessing her love for another. Shirley, who had no romantic prospects herself (unless you counted Mercator, who was sixty years old) thought MaryAnn was a stitch. "She's a little nervous," Shirley would explain, "but she's got a heart of gold." Actually, MaryAnn had a nasty little shriveled heart that would give her a lot of trouble in later years, but Shirley was one of those people who are continually surprised by the benevolence and charm of everyone they meet. She liked everybody. She was not a particularly good judge of character.

"So," Standish said, looking thrillingly into Shirley's eyes and using his most infallible opener, "I heard that you're the most interesting woman in the room."

"Excuse me?" said Shirley.

And that was the beginning of a whirlwind romance. Standish wined her and dined her. He took her to elevating concerts and amusing nightclubs. For the first time in her life, Shirley

Simon left the office every evening at 5 p.m. She got her nails done. She yawned in meetings. One day she had all the signs of a hangover. William Mercator, striding into her office one afternoon at 3, heard her whispering "kissed each finger and—" into the telephone. Hastily, and with a broken heart, he wheeled around and marched out. Three days later, she demurely requested a week off to get married. She said she had never been so happy. She had known Standish for a month and a half.

Standish was pretty happy, too. Granted, he had had to borrow some money for the wining and dining, but he figured he'd make it back in spades. He looked at himself in the mirror and sang, "Community property! Community property! Com-mun-it-eeeeeee prop-er-teeeeee!"

MaryAnn was confused. Never had she experienced such a thing. Shirley chosen over her? By this gorgeous man? "I don't get it," she said to her mirror, twisting her long, dark hair into an exotic arrangement. "Shirley?" She looked at herself for a long time, ruminatively stroking and plucking her smooth skin, and then she walked into her bedroom and picked up the phone. "Standish Lewall," she said into the receiver, "L-E-W-A-L-L. Yes, that's it. Thanks."

●

Several weeks went by in a flurry of wedding preparations. Shirley was momentarily perturbed by the concise nature of Standish's guest list: three people, one of whom was his cleaning lady. When she asked him about it, he looked at her with his round, innocent eyes and said, "I don't know very many people." She ran to embrace him, reproaching herself for having hurt his feelings. And besides, her list was long enough for both of them. Simons were gathering from far and wide; aunts, uncles, and cousins were flowing into the town's finest hotels in a steady stream. Old friends from camp, sorority sisters, neighbors from down the street—all were swarming toward the splendid nuptials of Shirley and Standish. Florists were gathering yellow roses ("Doesn't pink seem silly?" Standish murmured and Shirley cast an adoring look at her tasteful fiancé), bakers were concocting a triumvirate of towering cakes, and caterers were ejecting small explosions of caviar onto toast points. Shirley was scheduling her up-do, Shirley's mother was fussing about her shoes ("I said dyed to match, not dyed to almost match!"), and Shirley's young cousins were jumping on the hotel beds.

And in a coffee shop some blocks away, William Mercator was talking to a small man with a small camera. The man handed Mercator an envelope. Mercator handed the man a large wad of cash and walked gloomily toward Shirley Simon's apartment. Two hours later he left, only to return after a few moments, carrying a small paper bag containing several glue sticks.

●

"—**beautiful,** just beautiful," quavered Aunt Sophy Simon, kissing Shirley's cheek.

"You're a picture, my dear," intoned Bob Clark Black, an old family friend.

"He's a babe, Shirley," whispered Caralee, Shirley's cousin.

To each, Shirley mechanically smiled and nodded. Standish, next to her, beamed beatifically. Slightly farther down the receiving line, MaryAnn, as maid of honor, sustained a refined yet joyous smile that she had created especially for the occasion.

"Nice wedding," said a somewhat bedraggled woman in a red dress.

"Who are you?" Shirley asked.

"I'm Olive. His cleaning lady," she jerked her head toward Standish.

"You must know all his secrets," Shirley said in a flat voice.

Olive smiled grimly. "Yeah, I know 'em."

Standish intervened with a charming kiss, and Olive was passed down the receiving line. As the last guest trooped into the banquet room, Standish and Shirley and the grand wedding party seated themselves behind a sumptuous table, glittering with glassware and fine china. Soon, amidst the roar of hundreds, an insistent tapping on glass could be heard. Why, it was Shirley's brother Ben, who was Standish's best man, since Standish said he couldn't think of anyone he liked better. Ben gangled his way through a congratulatory speech and then completed the effect by spilling his champagne down the front of his pants. As the crowd guffawed, MaryAnn rose gracefully from her seat next to the bride and began to speak "I'd like to say a few words about Shirley, my dearest friend in the whole—"

Shirley rose suddenly to her feet. Her voice, purposeful and clear, drowned out MaryAnn's. "I think you're too nervous to talk, MaryAnn. You better sit down and let me do the talking, because I'm not nervous at all. I can tell you what MaryAnn was about to say, folks. I'm sure she was going to mention how long we have been friends. Right, MaryAnn? Ten years, that's how long. Ten years of me listening to her talk about all her boyfriends. Ten years of me picking her up from the airport after her weekend flings. Ten years of her canceling dinner with me if she got a date. What a friend. And here, over on the other side, is Standish. Stand up, Standish, and introduce yourself to these people. You don't know them, do you? Do you know anyone in the room? I think your cleaning lady left already, which really cuts down on your circle of loved ones. So this is Standish, everyone. Isn't he pretty? And this is me, standing between Standish and MaryAnn. They're both so pretty; maybe they should be together, shouldn't they? Of course, Standish just swore to love me until death do us part. Remember that bit? And the 'for richer' stuff? Well, never mind—just look at these two pretty people. I know you want to take a closer look, because they're so lovely. And I can help you get that closer look, because I made a party favor for each and every one of you. It's underneath your plates, friends—that's right, just turn your plates over and you can get a good look at these two pretty, pretty people."

At the bottom of every plate was pasted a photograph, and although the photo was small, the frenzied, naked bodies of Standish and MaryAnn appeared with startling clarity. They had apparently seen no need to close the bedroom curtains.

Shirley's mother screamed. Gasps filled the room. Ben began to giggle in high, embarrassed whinnies. Shirley's father shouted, "Why you sonofabitch, I'll kill you!"

Shirley walked calmly to the door, where William Mercator was waiting.

So**D**a **P**op

Well, the extra piece of pumpkin pie had been too much, that was clear. Stella's eyes flew open at 11:49, and there was no going back. She didn't feel good. Her stomach was gurgling and churning and swishing. Stella sighed and heaved herself out of the bed, which gave a soft sigh of expansion. She thudded down to the kitchen to get the bicarb.

The kitchen was the wrong place to be, and Stella tried not to look as she mixed a teaspoon of baking soda into a glass of water and gulped it down. She burped immediately. It was working. In the meantime, the leftover stuffing looked very tasty, and Stella thought she'd just have a spoonful. Not more, of course, with her stomachache. Besides, stuffing always tasted better the next day. Stella checked the clock on the wall. It was the next day. She helped herself to another spoonful. She caught a glimpse of MaryJo's bourbon balls in the cupboard when she replaced the soda, and took a few out of the tin and put them in her pocket. They would help her get back to sleep.

The funny thing was that they didn't, really. Stella looked at the ceiling for a long time, but she didn't feel sleepy. She felt sick. Her stomach was heaving and churning. She wondered if she was going to throw up. She hadn't thrown up in years, but she remembered that it was no fun. Maybe it was the green beans. Maybe they were bad, somehow. She hadn't really liked their almond dressing, though it had taken her several helpings to realize that. Or it could have been Marty's mashed yams, although they had seemed okay. But who knew, with Marty? She remembered the year he had put maraschino cherries in the yams. Nobody would eat them, and he got offended. MaryJo had said it was a crime against yams, and they had all laughed, even Marty. Her stomach was still in an

uproar. She was surprised it didn't wake Cyril up; he was such a light sleeper. She gave a little groan, to see if he would wake up and talk to her, but he didn't stir. All that fancy wine from Forrest's "cellar" had knocked him out. Stella looked at the clock—12:38, and still no relief. Maybe she needed more bicarb. She remembered hearing that the bigger the stomachache, the more soda it took.

The mattress gave its soft sigh again as Stella got out of bed. In the kitchen, she gave herself an extra large dose of soda, nearly two tablespoons, in a cup of water, and again, she burped gratifyingly as soon as she finished. The burp helped. The turkey was still sitting on the platter. An eighteen-pound bird. Very nicely done, if she did say so herself. She pinched a little meat off the bone and popped it into her mouth. She liked dark meat. In fact, her favorite part was the drumstick, which nobody else liked. She figured she could just go ahead and eat it now because Cyril certainly wasn't going to want it. There wasn't as much left this year; Patty had been pretty greedy about packing herself a plate of leftovers, but you couldn't blame her—she was such a bad cook herself that she had to eat up when she could. Those rolls of hers had been straight from the supermarket, prebaked, and even then, they didn't taste right. Stella picked one up. They were too doughy, almost uncooked inside. Stella took a big bite. They weren't inedible, but they weren't good. Jam helped a little. Stella had a couple more because bread was known to settle the stomach.

The stairs seemed too steep to climb again, so Stella lay down on the sofa. Her stomach began to ache sharply, but she didn't feel like she was going to throw up anymore, so the bicarb must have worked. She tried to think about other things. The cheese plate had been nice. The dip, too. She couldn't remember if there was any dip left. Phyllis said she had clipped the recipe out of the newspaper just last week; it was called Elegant Spinach Whirl, but it didn't taste like spinach at all. It was cream cheese, frozen spinach, sour cream, a touch of paprika, and something else. What? Stella wracked her brain—eggs? Oh, it was just driving her crazy. Stella heaved herself up and plodded back out to the kitchen irritably. Peering into the refrigerator, she found the extra dip and stuck her finger in it, but she couldn't tell. Could be eggs. She found some carrot sticks and dipped them one by one. Could be some other kind of cheese. Or maybe milk. Well, her stomach was no better at all. Maybe some more bicarb was in order. She remembered her father drinking a glass every day, "for health and wealth," he said, though the wealth part never happened. She tried to recall just how much he had taken. A lot, she was sure.

She sat down at the kitchen table with the baking soda box. She sprinkled about a quarter of a cup into a glass. That didn't look like enough to help. She put in another quarter of a cup. Well, it wasn't going to taste good, but maybe she'd find some relief. Her innards were roiling. A spoonful of sugar makes the medicine go down, she thought to herself, looking at Caroline's pecan pie. She cut herself just a sliver and filled the glass with water. It was hard to stir the thick glue of soda into a liquid, but eventually it was soupy enough to drink. She took a big swallow and almost gagged. Nastiest thing she had ever tasted. Gratefully, she ate a bite of pie. Caroline knew her pie, you had to say that for her. Stella thought nostalgically about a pumpkin pie that Caroline had made in 1976. Light enough to float. She took another giant gulp of soda and a quick chomp of pie. Better that way. You could almost forget the soda.

Slowly, alternating pie with bicarb, Stella got the whole glass down (it did take a second sliver of pie). Again, she burped satisfyingly afterward, and felt immediately better. A sudden craving for pickles swept over her; that was a good sign, she knew, because she always wanted pickles when she was ready to start fresh on something. Accordingly, she fished a few from the jar, and, munching, returned to the sofa. It creaked as she descended. She had heard that lying on your right side promoted digestion, so she rolled to her right, but her stomach felt as tight as a drum and it was just too uncomfortable, so she rolled back flat. Probably an old wives' tale anyway.

The gurglings of her intestines increased. She was glad Cyril was upstairs asleep, because the noise would surely have wakened him. Like boats rubbing together, it was.

Her stomach swelled as though for a giant burp, but none came, and it swelled again. Ohhh. This was the worst stomachache she had ever had, and she had had some bad ones. Maybe she would just go to sleep and wake up to find it was over. Stella tried determinedly to go to sleep, but she simply couldn't. About fifteen minutes later, she woke Cyril.

"Cy, honey, I think I'm in trouble here. My stomach is killing me."

"Mph. Yeah. Okay. Sorry," said Cyril, and fell back to sleep.

Stella lay across the bed, groaning, but Cyril didn't hear her. When her stomach finally burst within her from the expanding soda, the dull thud was too quiet to rouse him, and the sound of her deflating belly, like the soft hiss of a punctured tire, only lulled him deeper into sleep. It was only at 6:15 that Cyril awoke with an unaccountable craving for popovers.

the Perfect son-in-Law

We live in troubled times, I'll say that. People are more foolish now because they think they are less foolish. They talk on the phone, they send faxes, e-mails are flying through wires by the thousands. There are beepers, car phones, instant messages, e-zines, call waiting, chat rooms, and videograms, and no one has anything to say. All those ways to talk to each other, and the whole world is tongue-tied.

Take this girl; she was around twenty-five, I'll call her Sarah P. She had had all the education money could buy, right? Smart as a whip, good job as a researcher for an art library, not bad looking at all, with thick brown hair and high cheekbones. So she's full of information, knows things about art and politics, not hung up on this or that band of musicians like some girls her age. She's technologically literate, too, in a big way. All the older researchers are shook up because she's doing her job on a computer. She's talking HTML and URLs while they're looking at black-and-white pictures in books, and she's getting her job done quicker. The boss claps her on the back. She's a star. She's efficient, she's successful, and she's miserable.

It's love. She wants to love and be loved, like anyone else. But since she's so well informed and up-to-date, she reads all the important books and magazines, and they're all telling her a different way to be. Angry. Self-aware. Professional. Charming. Self-disciplined. Romantic. Edgy. Intuitive. Et cetera. Then she goes shopping or looks into one of those fashion magazines or, worse, looks at the television, and she sure doesn't look like those women, and those clothes look pretty bad on her, so she starts thinking that there's something the matter with her, even though she knows that the women in fashion magazines are ridiculous.

Then, boom! the second most attractive guy in the research department asks her out for a date. A date, okay, what's she supposed to do with that? How can she convey her personality in an appealing way? And just what is her personality anyway? And why should she have to put it on display for him? Is she so desperate? No! So the date happens, and she can't tell, is she being attractive? Is she attracted to him? They eat dinner and it's hard to think of things to talk about other than work, and even when they talk about work, they only say neutral things. And she feels like she should ask him something about his life, so she asks him where he grew up, and then she feels like a dope because they're talking about Iowa and she's saying things like "I've always wanted to go to Iowa," which is completely untrue and he knows it, but she can't think of anything else to say. So they keep on talking about where they grew up, and she tries to tell a funny story about her mother and father teaching her to drive and having a big fight, but when she gets to the part where she crashes the car into a tree, it doesn't sound so funny, and he just smiles and says, "That's funny." Ugh. She's sweating a little in her black turtleneck sweater. Finally, dinner is done. They're walking home, and then they come to her apartment building. Invite him in? How does she decide? So she asks him if he wants to come in for a glass of wine and then she feels like he feels like she's too eager. Ugh. But he comes in, and they're drinking their glasses of wine and he's saying how nice her apartment is, which it isn't, and then he puts his glass down on what is the only really good piece of furniture she owns and she's thinking, How neurotic would I look if I just casually got up and put a napkin under his glass? She stands up, but just at that second he says, "There's something I think I should tell you about myself," so she sits back down, trying to look attentive and like she hadn't gotten up at all. He tells her this long story about how his last girlfriend turned out to be a lesbian and he had been terribly hurt, and he just doesn't feel that he could make any kind of commitment at this time in his life although she (Sarah) is really great.

Thank God that's over, Sarah thinks when she shuts the door behind him. Then she thinks about how she's going to have to dry clean her black turtleneck.

She calls her mom.

"Why is it so hard, Mom?" she groans. "Why is it so impossible to meet someone interesting and to have a friendship based on the real stuff, like ideas and opinions?"

"Oh, honey, you'll meet someone. Of course you will. It's just that you young people have so many choices nowadays that you're in a state all the time. You all think you have so much power that you scare yourselves."

"Then what? Go back to no choices and get married at nineteen? I don't think so, Mom."

"That's what I did," her mother says quietly, "and I'm happy."

Sarah groans again, "I'm twenty-five and I've never met anyone I could stand to spend a week with!"

"What about that Bruno boy? You father says he's very nice."

"Jesus. No way I'm going to have Dad fix me up with some scion of Schenectady's great plumbing dynasty. Forget it."

"Okay, okay, have it your way," her mother replies, sighing.

"Where's Dad, anyway?" asks Sarah, trying to be conciliatory.

"Your father is online." Her mother sounds mildly irritated by this. "And he's been

online pretty much every waking moment since he got the new computer last Thursday. He says he's developing our vacation itinerary—doesn't that sound restful?—but I'm sure he's just playing."

"Honestly, he needs another hobby," says Sarah.

"I know. At least with golf he got some fresh air."

After a few more disparaging remarks about other members of the family and a pleasantry or two, they say goodnight. Sarah hangs up and rubs her eyes. I could watch TV, she thinks, but there's only grim news—"Promising young opera singer found decapitated today. More after this"—and a bulbous starlet opening slippery lips to grin at a talk-show host.

I should check my e-mail and go to bed, she thinks. So she sits down at the computer. Before you know it she's doodling around in a political chatroom. There are six participants and five of them are ganging up on this anti-abortion moron, which is like killing a mosquito with a cannon, but Sarah is interested in the way one guy, Rick, is laying out his argument. He's telling the moron just how moronic it is to oppose abortion while at the same time opposing funds for kids' social programs. Pretty soon the moron curses them all and calls it a night, but Sarah and Rick are in the midst of long exchange about education reform, which it turns out that they disagree about (Sarah is for local control, Rick is for federal standards), but in an interesting way. He's actually trying to persuade her, like a real debater, rather than repeating his position over and over, which is what most people do. And he's smart, too. Before the computers are turned off, they've exchanged e-mail addresses.

When Sarah accesses her e-mail the next day at lunch, there he is, with a barrage of articles and statistics about education attached. But they don't talk much about education because they get caught up in the validity of art criticism (subjective bunk or essential cultural tool?), and Sarah looks up guiltily at three o'clock and realizes that she hasn't done a lick of work since noon.

Now where do you think this is going? Of course. By the next week, they're spending hours online together each day. Yak yak yak. And by now it's getting personal. They're revealing ages, jobs, pasts. He's forty-five, which is pretty old in Sarah's book, but she decides not be close-minded. He says he retired after a windfall in the stock market, and Sarah accuses him of being a capitalist running dog, but he protests, citing extensive involvement in environmental causes. Sarah describes herself as an art historian, which leads to a long discussion about liberal arts majors, about which they are in absolute accord.

"He's witty, too," she says to her friend Maureen.

"Always a plus," says Maureen laconically. She doesn't approve of meeting people online.

"But it's the safest thing in the world," Sarah says.

"No. The safest thing in the world is never meeting anyone because men are scum," said Maureen.

"But there's no way I could be in physical danger, put it that way," says Sarah.

"He probably has a huge purple scar running down one cheek and can't go out in public. Or maybe he's got leprosy and one eye is sort of hanging down the side of his face."

"Oh Maureen, you're gross. And besides, this is a very good way not to get hung up on looks, right? It's a meeting of minds."

"Soon to be followed by a meeting of bodies, I'll bet you anything."

And, lo, the very next day, Rick suggests that they meet in person. "You're the most fascinating woman I've ever met," he writes, "except I've never met you."

Sarah's a little apprehensive. For one thing, he might very well have a huge purple scar running down one cheek, and then she'd have to face her own superficial attachment to attractiveness. The other, much more likely possibility is that, in person, they would be swamped by the date-ness of the occasion and feel compelled to engage in small talk She thinks she will just die of disappointment if their peculiar intimacy were replaced by awkward casualness. But he is so interesting, so opinionated, so passionate; it seems impossible that their conversation could ever be less than profound. She agrees to meet him.

He suggests the bar at the St. Regis, and she's impressed. He must have money. Drinks. 6:30. Tuesday. Despite its being a meeting of the minds, Sarah dresses very carefully that day—a scarf, even. She takes extra time with her makeup, too, but when one of the senior design guys says "Hey, you got a job interview or something?" she blushes horribly and goes into the bathroom to wash her face. She doesn't want to look like she's trying.

There's no mail from Rick, which makes the day pass very slowly. 3:30. 4:30. 5:30. At 6:00, Sarah leaps up from her desk, suddenly convinced she's going to be late. She gets stuck in traffic, and the taxi driver acts like he's never seen a twenty-dollar bill before, but finally, she's there. It's exactly 6:30. She walks into the bar and realizes that she doesn't know what to do. How does she find him? Ah, but there's the maitre d', tapping her on the arm. "Are you Sarah?" he murmurs discreetly. Rick has taken care of it. So thoughtful, she thinks as she walks through thick carpet, feeling a little dizzy. I could be about to meet the most important person in my life.

He's at one of the good tables, up on the balcony, and, with the waiter murmuring, "This way, Miss," she's walking toward his table. Toward him. He senses her approach and turns, smiling, to meet her.

Sarah's mouth goes dry at the same moment that the hair on the back of her head lifts. She gives him a long look. He's sixty, not forty-five. He's never had a windfall on the stockmarket. His name is Richard, not Rick.

"Hi, Dad," she says finally.

RAt food

NoW you know who I'm talking about, I know you do, but I'm not going to name names. Because they could get me good, that's why. They're rich rich rich, and you know, I'm lucky to have a dollar in my purse. They could send someone over here any day and that's the end of me. You wouldn't see me again.

Let me tell you. I'm sitting at one of their little plastic tables, minding my own business, eating my little bucket of fried chicken. I like the Tasty Tidbits bucket. You get a drumstick and a thigh and mash potatoes. You get coleslaw, too, but I don't care for coleslaw. Too sour. That time, I was reaching my fingers into my bucket, aiming to grab hold of the thigh. Now, I wasn't really paying attention—I was reaching for a napkin at the same time—but what my fingers pulled from that bucket was something long and thin and deep-fried. I about had a heart attack when I saw that thing waggling in the air. It was the tail of a rat, that's what it was, and after a minute, I thought to myself, If the tail's been deep-fried, you can bet the front of it got fried too. Then I looked real carefully in my bucket. They say it's a thigh, but how do we know? Could be a rat, easy.

Of course, I go to the counter, and it's Leonard Cummings up there, and I say, "Look what I found in my bucket, Leonard." He looks at it for a minute and says, "That's a rat tail." And I say, "You're right. What're you going to do about it?" and he offers me another bucket. I say that I'm not eating any more buckets ever again, and I want my $3.17 back.

And what does Leonard say? He says, "No ma'am, Miss Hill, I can't give you your money back."

So I start yelling and waving round the rat tail, and pretty soon everybody in the place is looking hard inside their buckets. "A paw! A paw!" screams one fellow, and then an old lady yells, "Looka here! This one's a rat for sure!" We gather round and yes sir, what she's got in her bucket is pretty near a whole rat, deep-fried. But now I take a good look, and her rat still has part of its tail. So it's a different rat!

We're all shouting now. Everybody wants their money back, and one poor girl just upchucks right there. What does Leonard Cummings do? He's just like his daddy, that boy—he calls the police on us! When it's his restaurant that's fed us rats!

When they came, I tried to show them the rat tail, but they paid me no mind. Get out of here, they said, or we'll arrest you for disturbing the peace. Me! A nice lady who goes to church every Sunday. That's what got me thinking that they're in cahoots—you know, mm-mm Chicken (I'm not saying it) and the government. Government probably knows all about the rats. I bet they're getting hush-money. I bet you anything.

the Flying Gypsy TRick

Once upon a time, a dreadful thing happened to a young man named Arthur Sheets. But then, dreadful things were always happening to Arthur Sheets. Even his infancy was rife with debacle: a snake came out of the garden hose and bit him when he was one and a half; he was sucked down the bathtub drain—at least his leg was—when he was two; and when he was four, he pushed a raisin up his nose and it got stuck. One time, he was sitting on a park bench, resting, and the bench suddenly fell into a deep hole. The sewer underneath the park had cracked, and the accumulation of water had created an underground sinkhole, all of which makes sense, but nonetheless, it didn't sink until Arthur got there. Arthur had bad luck with spaces.

For obvious reasons, Arthur grew up cautious. When he walked through a door, he stepped immediately to one side and stood against the wall. When he opened a can of soup, he stuck his finger in it to make sure there was nothing dangerous hiding in the noodles. He avoided storm drains at all costs. In bathrooms, even in his very own bathroom that he had used five million times, he always checked all sources of ingress or egress for untoward occupants or doubtful plumbing. What he did to toothpaste tubes is simply too disgusting to describe.

Arthur was not only cautious himself, he was a cause of caution in others. "Use your turn signal!" he would bellow from the sidewalk (Arthur did not drive himself, considering it a ridiculously dangerous activity), sometimes smacking the side of the car with his umbrella for emphasis. "Cirrhosis!" he would stage-whisper when he saw a customer emerging from a liquor store. Occasionally, he popped his head into a restaurant to call out, "Ninety percent of Hepatitis B cases come from food service workers failing to wash their hands after going to the bathroom."

Adults were bad enough, but children drove him crazy. Dark personal experience had taught him that children were far more accident prone than grown-ups, but, as a group, children were also far more resistant to safety rules. Accordingly, where Arthur settled for exhortation with adults, he took action with children. He wrenched lollipops from their lips if they were walking; he clung to their legs if they were climbing trees; he issued ringworm ointment if they were barefoot; and he checked the brakes on every stroller he came across.

Mothers, he felt, were impossibly lax when it came to strollers. "You think he's safe because you fastened the belt," he would begin, approaching a young mother pushing a stroller, "but I have seen with my own eyes a stroller collapse inward, crushing the ribcage of the baby within!" Often, by this time, the mother was sprinting away, so Arthur would have to shriek his denouement. "The baby DIED! You should get that child a helmet if you're going to run so fast!"

Sad to say, Arthur was not a popular person. In fact, he had not a single friend. He had had one, but then they went to a restaurant together and when Arthur was finished looking under the table, his friend was gone. Arthur had had to take a taxi home, which was horrible because he had wrapped his face in his scarf to repel germs and the taxi driver thought he was being robbed at gunpoint and, well, it was a problem. Anyway, Arthur never saw that friend again, which, Arthur said, was the last straw. Lacking companions, Arthur devoted himself to his family. Not his actual family, whom he felt to be criminally negligent ("How could you have given me a raisin in the first place?" he had shouted at his mother), not to mention unsanitary, uncouth, and unsympathetic, but his family of correspondents. Arthur was a pen pal extraordinaire; he had seventeen correspondents in twelve different countries. He didn't accept pen pals from countries with diseases that could conceivably be transferable by letter, but that left a lot of nice European countries, particularly the northern ones. His most daring correspondence was with a Greek woman; not only because of the questionable germs of Greece, but because he had allowed his letters to touch lightly on the subject of romance. It was really quite gratifying how Iphigenia had responded to his hints. Their exchange had grown, Arthur told himself, rather heated.

"The pen," he muttered to himself, "is mightier than the sword." He looked contemptuously at a robust businessman driving a sport utility vehicle. "You are exceeding the speed limit," he said, but not loudly; he didn't want to break his mood. Love was in the air, he thought to himself, composing that night's epistle to Iphigenia.

As time went on, Arthur grew more and more bold. "You are the shadowy nightingale whose song drifts in my window in the still blue night," he wrote. "I yearn simply to sit in your presence." Iphigenia replied in kind. "I dream of your arrival on dawn's rosy fingers," she wrote. Furthermore, she sent a photo; she had thick dark hair and arching eyebrows. She was beautiful.

Finally, destiny struck: she invited him to visit her. At first, Arthur was appalled. Go to a dirty little Greek island probably roiling with vermin? Was she mad? But, after long hours of consideration and repeated glances at the photo, Arthur began to develop the criteria under which such a visit could be made. He made lists of hygiene protocols and acceptable foods; he drew up plans for transportation that would reduce his exposure to Greece to a tolerable level; and he developed a roster of items that he would need to ship over before his arrival, such as his bed. It took him a week of calculation, but in the end he acquiesced to Iphigenia's invitation, including photocopies of all his lists and plans in his letter of acceptance. He began to call the cruise lines (there would, of course, be no flying in airplanes) to inquire about costs.

But, from Iphigenia, there was silence. Two weeks, three weeks, went by, and Arthur heard nothing. He fumed at the Greek postal system, and, summoning his reserves, ventured again to the photocopy store, and reposted all his documents, including his letter. Two weeks, three weeks—nothing. Now Arthur fumed at Iphigenia; "Faithless woman!" he muttered, shaking his umbrella at passing cars. All too soon, though, his rage faded to heartbreak. He spent hours looking at her lovely picture, his hand clasped over his heart. In the grocery store, he burst into tears at the sight of the peas, which Iphigenia had told him were her favorite vegetable. A few days later, the mere thought of peas caused tears to dribble down his cheeks. "I am a man betrayed," he whispered to himself over and over, not even noticing the nervous glances of his fellow subway passengers. Then a thought struck him. "Am I a man or a mouse?" he exclaimed. The woman on the seat beside him got up and stood by the door. "I've been wasting my time! I must reclaim her! Yes! Of course! Why didn't I think of it sooner!" By this time there were quite a few empty seats around Arthur, so he looked in vain for someone to tell of his discovery. Finally, he shouted over several rows of seats to a tired-looking woman with a broken purse, "I'm going to Greece to win back my love!"

She looked at him. "Maybe you should get off this train and call your travel agent when we get to the next station."

"You are so right!" Arthur said enthusiastically.

Not a week later, he was on the boat to Greece, meticulously sorting and cataloguing his packets of food, inspecting his first-aid kit, and doing aerobics. When he could find a moment, he inspected All the Greek You Need, a handy laminated sheet of useful phrases. At night, he read *The Romance of the Aegean*, which he thought was going to be about love, but turned out to be about fishing When he arrived at Piraieus, his careful study of the transit maps paid off, and he was at the Athens train station in half an hour. It was there that his troubles began. Though he tried, really tried, to ignore the flies crawling on bread, the pungent smell of sweat and oil, and the spectacle of boys leaping over the tracks from one train to another, Arthur began to feel a pulse of pure terror lighting his veins. Shouts, spittle, train whistles, little children running around underfoot, all of it taking place at a speed that made him dizzy. Arthur tried vainly to concentrate on the schedule. "Next train for Naplion," he muttered feverishly, while the tiny numbers swam before his eyes. A sudden squawk from a loudspeaker over his head made him jump; a torrent of high-volume Greek poured forth, which passersby showed no signs of hearing. Dragging the little wheeled carriage that contained his luggage behind him, Arthur floundered toward the platform that held, he hoped, the train to Naplion. Once there, he would have to catch another boat to Kithnos. And then a bus—the thought was horrible—to Iphigenia's home in Gastouni. He began to sweat profusely, and his coat flapped damply behind him as he approached the train.

"Is this the train for Naplion?" he called out foolishly to passing Greeks. A few turned to smile at him, but none replied, because they had no idea what he was saying. A passel of

Germans thumped past, with their bulging, dirty backpacks slamming against their sturdy backs. "Naplion? Naplion!?" he cried. The train began to lurch ever so slightly forward, but Arthur could not bring himself to board it without knowing that it was the correct train. Young men rushed by and heaved themselves into welcoming hands and were hauled aboard. There was one last earsplitting whistle, and the train gathered speed and burst out of the station. Arthur was alone with his luggage on the platform.

That's when it happened: from farther down the track, a group of slight, dark-haired people began to walk toward him. They laughed and called to one another, and Arthur felt for a moment that they would help him. As he looked at them, he realized two things: that they were Gypsies, and that they were walking oddly, in formation almost. He began to feel afraid, and just as he began to feel afraid, they began to run. They were running right at him, shouting and whooping, and Arthur couldn't figure it out. What were they doing? What did they mean? His body wanted to run away, but his legs were paralyzed. As they ran, the group parted, and Arthur saw that in the middle was a man carrying a baby, a little baby whose red face was contracted into a squall of anger and fear. That's how I feel, Arthur thought, just as the man lobbed the baby in a quick underhand directly at Arthur's chest. There was a moment in which Arthur saw the baby, a compact bundle hurtling through the air, and saw the Gypsies racing toward him, and he realized that his luggage and his wallet were as good as gone. But the habit of a lifetime could not be broken, and Arthur lifted his hands to receive the baby dropping from the sky. It fell like an apple into the safety of his arms, and for the first time that he could remember, Arthur felt like he had actually rescued someone. The Gypsies were swarming over him; he could feel hands slithering into his pockets and the bulge of his wallet disappearing. They were yelling and calling to one another, and an old man with a face like an ancient shoe was easing the baby out of Arthur's arms. Unexpectedly, both for the old man and for Arthur, Arthur resisted. He pulled the baby away from the old man and held it tight. Three men were disappearing with one of his suitcases down the platform, and the other two bags had already vanished, seemingly melted away. There were just two of the band left; clearly, their job was to retrieve the baby. They jostled Arthur and pulled at his arms, shouting, but Arthur jerked away.

"GET AWAY FROM ME! " he shrieked, yanking the baby back toward his chest. "THIS IS MY BABY. MINE, MINE, MINE!" And Arthur began to run as he had never run before. Every child that he had ever warned, or admonished, or tried to help was wrapped inside this baby, and he knew that he could save it. He ran and ran and ran, and finally, as he reached the crowded center of the station, where policemen with automatic weapons slung casually over their shoulders were lounging in doorways, his pursuers drifted away. Panting, out of breath, sweating profusely, Arthur slowed to a walk. He had forgotten for a second, in the excitement of the chase, that he held a baby. When he looked down, the baby looked up—and began to laugh.

"Hello baby," said Arthur tenderly. "Let's go get us a nice plane ticket home."

Thicker
than WATER

Brooks Archer stirred impatiently in his chair. It was hard for him to keep his mind on the meeting. What were they blabbing about? Oh, what to name the new E3.

"Colara. I don't like it. Sounds like a drink, not a car."

"Solara," said Taylor Coats.

"Toyota's already got it. Jeez, don't you read the literature?"

"Sorry," said Taylor.

"Let's see, Dolara, Folara, Golara, Holara—ha, that's good—Jolara, K—no—Lolara, Molara, Nolara, Polara. Polara. What about that?" exclaimed Tyler Burnright enthusiastically. Brooks groaned inside. Tyler was an idiot.

Sanders Fifing, the CEO, suddenly boomed, "Did we or did we not pay Asto and Gett seven-hundred-fifty thousand dollars to find us a name for this damn car?"

"We did," said Tyler, abashed.

"Then why are you sitting here playing with the goddamn ALPHABET?!" Fifing's heavy fist pounded the table.

"Sorry, Sanders."

"Tell them we goddamn don't like Colara and we expect them to find us a new one goddamn immediately."

"You got it, sir," said Tyler.

Brooks was imagining the speech. "And finally, of course, we must honor the man who changed the course of history in a single day, Brooks Archer. Leading a team of researchers into the realms of the unimaginable, he scaled the Everest of scientific conundrums and emerged victorious. But I would remind you, ladies and gentlemen, that Brooks Archer has made all of us victors. Victors over greed, strife, environmental disaster, and despair. It is with the greatest pleasure and the greatest respect that I announce that Brooks Archer has made history yet again, as the first man to win both the Nobel Peace Prize and the Nobel Prize for Chemistry." The hum grew to a roar, and as he began to walk towards the stage, the audience rose to its feet. Hmm. He realized that he was confusing the Nobel Prize with the Academy Awards. Maybe there wasn't a stage—he'd have to rethink that part.

"What's next?" growled Sanders.

Mimi looked at her list. "Mr. Archer put an item on the agenda, sir. He said it was about water, but that's all he would say." She looked primly at Brooks.

"Water? What the hell does that mean, Archer?"

interesting development. A very interesting development. It seems to me that we have a truly unique opportunity to position ourselves at the front of a movement. This is the dawn of a new age, and I know you'll agree with me when I say that there's no company more deserving of this moment than ours. With you, Sanders, at the helm to guide us—"

"WHAT?" The veins on Sanders's neck were popping out.

"Oh. Sorry," said Brooks, "They've got an engine that runs on water. Just—water. Use it the same way you use gasoline, but it's clean, you know, because it, um, doesn't, you know, burn." He blushed. He was making a hash of this. "It's like a little hydroelectric system. In theory, anyway, the catalytic—"

"It's a theory? Or do they have a working prototype?" Sanders leaned across the table, his face impassive.

"Oh no, sir, they've got a prototype. I mean, it works. I saw it."

"And it fits in the same space as an engine?"

"Well, yeah, because you can take out the radiator, so even if it's a little bigger, it's still—"

"Okay, okay. Give me a minute here." For the first time in twenty-five years, Brooks saw Sanders look confused. He stared at the table for several minutes. Finally, he spoke. "How many people know about this?"

"Well," Brooks thought for a moment, "everybody down there knows, so that's about forty people. They're pretty excited about it. And I guess my secretary knows. And now all of you." He smiled in what he hoped was a way that let Sanders know that he was the catalyst behind the whole project.

There was a long silence.

"How much does a researcher make?" asked Sanders.

"Oh gosh. Um. About $125,000, I guess, on average."

"Okay, here's what we're going to do, Archer. We're going to give every single person in Research a bonus of $500,000. This bonus has nothing—nothing at all, do I make myself clear?—with any product that may have been developed at any time during the history of the research department. You, Archer, will immediately, as in tonight, requisition all paperwork pertaining to this so-called engine and you will give it to me. You will inform the research department that this—this water project," Sanders pronounced the words with revulsion, "will be defunct as of today. If, for any reason or at any time, a researcher associated with this project resigns, I must be informed immediately. Do I make myself clear? " Sanders gathered his papers briskly.

"But Sanders. Greed, strife, environmental disaster," Brooks said weakly.

Sanders looked down at him with what in any other person would be called pity. "Money," he said. Then he turned. "Tyler, set up a conference call with Lee and Noburo and Jim and Marty. I'll tell them what we're up against. Water. Jesus. We've got to hold the line on this one." He stood up and his eyes rested on Brooks. "Thanks for bringing this matter to my attention, Archer. You've done the right thing." He strode briskly from the boardroom, Tyler and Taylor marching at his heels. "Water. Jesus. The stocks would go to shit. Jesus."

Fiat Lux

"**Now,** it's important to remember that you have to stop at all intersections where you cannot see one hundred feet in either direction, whether a Stop sign is posted or not," said Francis Frydeger, fingering his keys.

"Right," said Fiona.

"And at all railroad crossings."

"Only if you're driving a bus," said Fiona.

"Don't argue with me, young lady, or the lesson's over," snapped Francis. "And you must always ask all your passengers if their seat belts are securely fastened."

"But Dad, I can see that your seat belt is securely fastened."

"Aha!" crowed Francis, "You think you can see that my seat belt is securely fastened—but it's not!" He unsnapped his seat belt with a flourish. "You are responsible for the lives of your passengers, Fiona. Perhaps you are not aware of that. " Francis picked a piece of lint off his shirt pocket.

"I'm aware of it," said Fiona sullenly. "Can I start the car?" They had been in the garage for more than an hour.

Francis rolled his keys between his fingers. "In Washington, D.C., you may not park within one hundred feet of a corner, regardless of the color of the curb."

Fiona swallowed. "Dad," she said in strangled voice, "we don't live in Washington, D.C. Can I start the car?"

"I don't know, Fiona. Can you?"

"May I?"

"Yes. It's the gold key." He dangled it in front of her. "Now, warming up your engine is a critical but often overlooked component of car maintenance. Perhaps you don't realize it, Fiona, but metal fatigue, which is caused by insufficient warm-up, is one of the leading causes of premature automotive failure. Each and every time you start the car, you must let the engine run for a minimum of three minutes. Do I make myself clear?"

"Uh-huh."

"Now, simply insert the key into the ignition." For some reason, Francis crooked his fingers into imaginary quotation marks around the word ignition. "You need to be very careful not to over-turn the starter. Turn the key to here and let go. Yes. Let me see you do it one more time."

Sighing, Fiona restarted the car.

"Fine. Now, you need to be in reverse. Do you understand why?"

Fiona looked at him dully. "Because if I'm not in reverse, we'll drive into that wall."

"Exactly!" said Francis with triumph. "Reverse is indicated by this R." He pointed it out with his index finger. "Simply depress the button here, and glide the gear shift into the slot next to the R. See?"

"Yes."

"Now, you must always remember to check your mirrors once every fifteen seconds. When you're in reverse, of course, you need look into your rearview mirror as if it was the windshield. Check your side mirrors. That's right. Both sides. Now, take a quick glance to the front."

"Dad, we're in the garage. Why do I have to check the front?"

"No backtalk! To get you into your safety-first mode, that's why."

"Oh."

Slowly, amidst a shower of instructions, Fiona backed out of the driveway and inched her way down the street.

"STOP!" shrieked Francis.

Fiona threw her entire weight on the brake and the car lurched forward. "What? What?" she cried.

"There's a Stop sign ahead," Francis yelped, pointing.

"Dad! The Stop sign is at the corner. We're in the middle of the block. Jeez."

"Don't you roll your eyes at me, young lady. I was testing your reflexes. Which is very important, though you probably don't realize it. Now, Fiona, pedestrians have the right of way at all intersections, whether they are marked with a crosswalk or not. Should you come to a Stop sign at the same time as another car, the one on the right takes precedence. And here's a little known fact: if a fire engine, a police car, an ambulance, and a mail truck come to a four-way intersection at the same time, the mail truck gets to go first. I'll bet you didn't know that."

"Uh huh," said Fiona, concentrating.

"You must yield to uphill traffic when you are coming down a narrow road."

"Hmmm."

"You must stop one hundred yards behind a school bus with flashing red lights."

"Uh," said Fiona.

"FIONA!"

Once again, the car lurched to a stop.

"What?" cried Fiona.

"Are you paying attention to me?"

Lurching and rolling, they worked their way several miles into town. Teaching is my métier, thought Francis fondly. He congratulated himself on giving instructions so clearly that even a teenager could understand them. I have a rapport with youth, he mused. I always have. Shelley, for example, the receptionist in the office next door. Hadn't she just been telling him that they had a rapport? "I wish I could work for someone like you," she had said, fingering his letter opener coyly. "Your office is so much nicer than Doctor Goldberg's. All those colons. Yuck." Yes, young people were attracted to him—or not so much him, he thought modestly, but his authority. His competence. Young people had so little direction. They looked to older men, like him, to model a commitment to goals. I should do more charity work, he thought. Teach one of those leadership camps for inner-city youth, like Lindermayer. Lindermayer was a pain in the ass. Wouldn't shut up about the damn underprivileged. I did this, I did that, I'm such a hero. It'd be a kick in the

pants to tell him he's not the only one who's onto the underprivileged. Francis chuckled.

"What?" said Fiona.

Francis snapped to attention. Somehow, while he had been thinking, darkness had fallen. "Turn on your headlights!" he commanded.

"I did it already," Fiona said.

"Not your parking lights, mind you, and not your high beams. The notch right in the middle there."

"That's the one I've got on, Daddy."

"It's illegal to drive with your parking lights on, and your high beams can only be used when you are alone on the road. You must dim your high beams when you approach within one hundred yards of another car."

"I know."

Francis had a thought. "However, you may flick your high beams, like this," he wiggled his finger, "to alert another driver that he has forgotten to turn on his headlights."

"Oh, no, Daddy, nobody does that anymore, because—"

"A case in point, Fiona!" bellowed Francis, feeling that destiny was on his side. A dark car was driving slowly toward them. "Flash your brights!"

"Daddy," Fiona said urgently, "You don't do that anymore—"

"It's almost past us! Flash, flash!" shrieked Francis.

"Daddy, I can't! It's a gang initiation rite!" The car passed them. "They drive around with their lights off, and if you flash your lights at them, they shoot your car. Really!"

Francis paused to collect himself.

"You may not realize it, Daddy, but flashing your high beams can be injurious, even fatal," Fiona said with a tiny smile.

It was the smile that enraged him. "You just button your lip, young lady!" Francis shouted, slamming his fist against the dashboard. "Don't think you can make a fool of me! Gang initiation rite, indeed! I wasn't born yesterday, and if you think that being an ungrateful snip is the way to get more driving lessons from me then you've got another think coming!"

"Daddy, I was just—"

"You were just lying to me! Gang initiation rite! When I tell you to flash your high beams, you flash them. Do you hear me?"

"I won't! I'll get shot!"

"Don't give me that!"

Another dark car was approaching stealthily. Francis did not stop to consider the statistical likelihood of two unlighted cars driving through the same city street in such close proximity. He merely lunged for the stem that controlled the headlights and flicked it wildly back and forth as Fiona screamed "No, no, no!" Wildly she grappled with her seat belt and succeeded in dropping to the floor as a hail of gunfire shattered her windshield. As the dark car glided by theirs, she heard a low chuckle.

"Thanks," a rich voice said.

Francis, his seat belt securely fastened, was killed immediately.

the ORgan PLAYer

It happened to a young man named Stanislas Charjatisc-Barjovsky, but aside from his name, he was completely average. You would have to look for a long time before you found anyone more average than he was. His friends called him Stan, of course, and he lived in an ugly, but not unbelievably ugly, apartment. It was just ugly in the regular way that guys' apartments are, with furniture that nobody else wanted and not very much of it. When Stan came home after a long day of school (he studied ergonomics) and work (he was a caddy), he would fling himself onto his defeated-looking green-and-brown plaid couch, open a beer, and watch TV. When he needed a change, he would meet his friends at a bar and watch TV there. Sometimes—not very often—he went out with a girl. These were sobering occasions for Stan; the girl always seemed to be waiting for him to say something, and he couldn't for the life of him figure out what that thing might be. In this manner, several years passed. Stan saw no reason why anything in his life should ever change. At the very same time, he imagined his future self as the possessor of a clean and stately house, a large automobile, and an athletic and agreeable wife.

Everything began normally on the day it happened. Stan was a little late to class because he had spent a lot of time trying to figure out which of his dirty shirts was the least dirty. Not that it really mattered, but there was a kind of cute girl in Elements of Physical Education, and he was thinking about asking her out maybe later in the year. So he was late to class, and the professor said, "Thank you for clearing time in your busy schedule to be with us, Mr. Charjatisc-Barjovsky." The class tittered, especially the cute girl, and then Stan sort of fell when he was trying to sit down at a desk, which was one of those stupid ones you had to slide into, and this time no one laughed, they just looked away. He had forgotten to bring money for lunch, and when he borrowed five dollars from his friend Gary, he realized

that he had to save two dollars for the bus to work and that the only thing he could afford was a hot dog. So he ate the hot dog, but he was still hungry, so he thought to hell with it and spent the other two dollars on a piece of pizza, which turned out to be gross. He thought he would find Gary and get some more money, but Gary had gone to class. So then he saw Pete, but Pete said "Sorry, dude, no cash." Nobody else he knew walked by, except the cute girl from Elements of Physical Education, and he sure wasn't going to ask her for two dollars. All of this took a lot of time, and when Stan finally realized that he was going to have to walk all the way to the golf course, he also realized that he was going to be late.

The golf course was, contrary to tradition and reason, on the top of a hill. Actually, it was sort of a mesa, but still, you had to walk uphill to get to it. Two miles uphill, plus two miles from the campus to the beginning of the hill, which meant at least an hour even if you ran, which Stan couldn't manage the whole way. By the time he got there he was pretty sweaty.

Also, he was in big trouble. Tom Smiles, who ran the pro shop, was already a caddy short because Big Mike had gone on a bender on Tuesday, and Tom was pissed. There were two fat cats waiting, and they weren't too happy either. The rain held off until they were at the third hole, but the fat cats turned out to be chest-thumpers, and so Stan had to walk the whole course in the rain with two sodden bags thumping against his thighs. It was 7:30 before they pressed their precision-calculated tips into his palm and left. Stan tried to snag some venison steak from the kitchen, but Manuel told him to get his ass the hell out of there or he'd stick a spatula in it, so Stan began the long walk downhill. His ugly apartment was four-and-a-half miles away. He was hungry and it was dark, so when a pair of bright head-lights cut across the road, disappeared, and then flashed around the curve toward him, he stopped and put out his thumb. The car pulled over the wet gravel, and the window rolled down. A cadaverously thin man with a withered face stared at Stan for a few seconds, and then reached over to unlock the door.

"You going toward town?" the man asked.

"Yeah. Town. Arapaho Street, if you're going that way." Stan sat down, dripping water on the seat.

"That's exactly where I'm going," the man said with a giggle.

In the wavering, pallid light of the road they traveled in silence for a few minutes. Then the man reached out a spidery hand to Stan. "Want some?" He held a bottle of tequila.

"Uh. Thanks, dude, but I can't drink that stuff."

"No?" said the man curiously. His smile was extraordinarily wide. There was some-thing the matter with his nose, too, Stan noticed. It looked as though one nostril had grown shut. "That's smart. It's bad for you." The man giggled. "I bet you'd like a beer, though."

"Well, yeah, I can drink a few beers." Stan didn't know whether this was an occa-sion for large claims. He decided it was. "As a matter of fact, I can drink a pretty fair number of beers. Some guys I know get all squirrelly after, like, two beers, but I can hang in there.

There's this one dude I know, he's practically unconscious after a pint, and, like, one night we had to take him home because he was all ahhhhg. He's a pussy—"

"Want a beer?" The spidery man interrupted rudely.

Stan didn't know what to say. Was the guy, like, inviting him to a bar? Maybe he was a homo or something. "Whoa, yeah, dude," he said nervously.

The man squealed the car to a stop in the middle of the road and bent down, groping under his seat. After a few moments, he pulled out a sweating cold bottle of beer. "Here. Home-brewed. Made it myself."

Stan would have preferred a Budweiser, but he popped it open and took a loud gulp. "Hey. Not bad. Nice and cold, anyway."

"Yes." There was a short silence. "I like to keep things cold." At this, he began to giggle so wildly that the car nearly veered into a ditch.

When his eyes clicked open Stan figured he was blind because it was so dark. My eyes are gone, he thought, and for several minutes, that seemed reasonable. Thoughts were struggling out of a tiny hole in the middle of his brain; they came slowly, very slowly. If I can blink, I still have eyes, he thought. He blinked. A new thought was coming, but it took a long, long time. I am very cold. I am very cold. He thought this several times before he realized that he was colder than he'd ever been in his life. A time passed before he identified the stuff he was sitting in as ice. Why am I sitting in ice, he wondered. That, too, took a few minutes to sink in. I should get up. Yes. Here are my hands. Here is my face. I am very cold. I should get up. Out of the ice. Stan reached out his hands and discovered thick porcelain walls. This is something, he thought, but what? A bathtub. He felt glad that he had figured that out. If it's a bathtub, I can get out of it. He remembered that people put their hands on each side of the tub and pushed up from their feet. This seemed plausible, and after awhile, Stan placed his hands on the sides of the tub. He began to heave himself forward, but his freezing legs had not received his instructions and he slipped down further into the ice. Hypothermia. His brain produced this word spontaneously, and Stan was impressed. I will die if I cannot get out of this tub, he told himself seriously. He wiggled his toes to prepare his feet and tried once more. This time, his legs pulled under his body obediently, and at that instant Stan felt a shivering, ripping, bursting slash of pain in his back. His first thought was that an animal was eating him, and then he fainted, pitching forward into the ice. This was lucky, for the cold revived him before he drowned. Stan began to scream helplessly in the dark.

A long time or maybe only a few minutes later, someone opened the door and Stan saw that he was in a bathroom.

"Shut up, shut up, shut up, what, shut up, shut up," said a nervous-sounding woman as she switched on the light. "You shut up in my hotel, you. The people are sleeping, they're calling, they're saying someone's screaming, screaming—Aaaaa!" she yelled, catching sight of the blood-filled bathtub. She continued yelling as she saw the oozing slash in Stan's back, crossed with awkward black stitches.

Three hours later, Stan was resting on the stiff white sheets of a hospital bed. Small, soothing beeps resounded through the halls, and nurses walked this way and that with reassuring rubbery treads. Doctor Lee smiled sympathetically down at him. "Put it this way, Stan; it's nice to have two kidneys, but you really only need one." She laughed in a comforting way. "And even if the police do find the people who stole your kidney, I don't think we'll be putting it back in. Ha ha."

"Ha, ha," said Stan politely, and then he burst out, "Why me? How could this happen? This isn't what happens!"

"Oh Stan," Dr. Lee said kindly, "Certainly it happens; you just don't hear about it very often because people are scared to talk."

"Why? Why scared?" asked Stan nervously.

"Well, Stan, if these criminals are sick enough to steal your organs, think what they'd do if they thought they might get caught." She shook her head wisely.

"Oh. Gosh," said Stan. He reflected on that for a moment. "But why me, Dr. Lee? Why did they choose me?"

"Stan, it's because you're an average guy, young, in good health, without a family. They've probably had their eyes on you for a long time." This time she nodded her head.

In spite of himself, Stan felt a little proud. It was kind of like winning a contest. Dr. Lee patted his arm pleasantly and told him to rest. He did.

The good thing about the hospital was that there was plenty to eat. Stan stocked up, because he knew there wasn't anything in the refrigerator at his apartment. The police came to talk to him, which was interesting. And there was a TV aimed right at his bed. Stan had a fine time at the hospital, but after three days, they told him to go home.

Gary said he would pick Stan up ("Whoa, kidney thieves! Wild!" he had said enthusiastically when Stan called him), but Gary was late, as usual, so Stan cooled his heels in the lobby, waiting. He watched the kindly old ladies at the reception desk giving people bad directions and grim-faced doctors hurrying toward the elevators. New mothers limped past with tiny, squalling bundles, and clusters of visitors, gloomy or celebratory, moved in phalanxes across the carpet. Stan stared dispassionately at a small girl having a tantrum in the gift shop; he thought her mother was probably going to smack her pretty soon. Then he heard a giggle. It was far away, across the lobby. Where did I hear that before, thought Stan. Oh, I remember. In the car.

He jerked his head up and scanned the vast space, looking for the spidery man. Nothing. But then, another giggle. And there, past the reception desk, standing in the door of the cafeteria, wearing surgical scrubs, stood the spidery man with the withered face. His head was turned in conversation with another figure, but even from this distance, Stan could see the strange closed nostril. And the giggle was unmistakable. He was laughing uproariously now, and the other figure began to laugh, too. She threw back her head at the joke, and Stan recognized Dr. Lee, her sympathetic face distorted with laughter.

when in Rome

We went to about five hundred churches and a thousand museums. Mom would read to us from the guidebook before we went in, so we would be sure to appreciate the right things, but they all looked pretty much the same to me. All the churches had coffins with old body parts in them, which was supposed to be some sort of miracle, I don't know why. My favorite was in Siena, where they had a little gray thumb on a stick. A sign said it was St. Catherine's. All I could think of was the person who cut it off—was it his job or something, cutting up saints? All the museums had the same pictures in them: Jesus being born or Jesus getting crucified.

Mom and Dad were in paradise, though. "There it is! There it is!" they gasped every time they saw an old building. You should have seen them in the Sistine Chapel; they were so excited they couldn't hold still. They ran up and down the floor with their fingers in the air, pointing. Every night, when he tasted his dinner, Dad would close his eyes and kiss his fingers and say "Benissime!" And when the sun set, he and Mom would lean back in their chairs and say, "Ahh, the light!" It was really kind of cute.

Granny didn't think so. Granny hated Italy. "It smells like sweaty men," she said, every single day. Back in Connecticut, you should have heard her sniffing about how she had never been anywhere since she went to Tampa for her honeymoon and how she supposed that it was her fate to have children who were globetrotters and left her at home to do the chores. Finally, she just wore Mom down. But from the minute she got on the plane, she hated it. "You didn't tell me it would take so long," she said to Mom. Mom just sighed. Granny thought the hotels were unsanitary and she said that the water was poisoning her. What she really hated were Italians. The fact that they didn't speak English drove her crazy. In Orvieto we went to one of those big outdoor markets where they were selling vegetables and flowers and stuff, and Granny kept asking people for an iced tea. They would look at her and shrug and she got madder and madder. When Mom whispered that they didn't understand her, Granny blew a gasket. "Everyone knows what an iced tea is, Elizabeth. Everyone. These people don't fool me! They're just rude. RUDE. RUDE. RUDE." By the end, she was screaming. The people in the stalls were fascinated, and I can't blame them. Granny looked pretty wild.

"Mia madre non sta bene," my Mom said, patting Granny on the arm. "Mother, let's go and sit down. Maybe we can find some juice or something."

"I don't want juice. I want an iced tea! What kind of a country doesn't have iced tea?" Granny was still yelling. It would have been funny, but I felt sorry for Mom. My sister, Jana, who's

thirteen and terminally embarrassed, was pretending to be enthralled by some tomatoes in a bin. She was hoping that people would think she was eighteen and travelling alone through Europe. Everywhere we went, she walked about seven paces behind us, trying to look like she just happened to be near this weird family and she herself was an orphan. I really think Mom and Dad should have left Jana at home with Granny, but of course nobody asked my opinion.

After the iced tea incident, Granny wouldn't get out of the car (except to eat). We'd drive three hours to see some big-deal mosaic or fresco, and when we got there, Granny would say, "It doesn't sound like much to me. I'm staying in the car."

"You're going to get pretty hot, staying in the car. Why don't you come in?" Mom would say.

"I'll open a window."

"Come on, Mother. It's supposed to be beautiful. Listen. 'Built in the latter half of the third century—"

"Elizabeth, when I'm senile, you can drag me from pillar to post. For now, I'll decide where I'll go and where I won't go, thank you very much." Granny put her purse in her lap and folded her arms over it, like she was resisting arrest.

After a minute, Mom just turned around and went, but you could tell it took some of the fun out of her trip, Granny being so miserable.

We were in Assisi when it happened. Mom was thinking that if anything was going to stop Granny from moping, Assisi would be it. Everyone likes St. Francis because he was such a nice guy to the animals and gave all his clothes away to the poor. Mom thought that even Granny would be interested in St. Francis. Wrong. Granny said she wanted to stay in the motel (that's what she called the pensiones, which weren't like motels at all) and have a Pepsi. So we found her a Pepsi and walked over to the big old church, which was pretty neat, I have to admit. They didn't have any shriveled pieces of St. Francis, but they had a lot of shriveled pieces of his friend St. Clare.

Anyway, the long and short of it is that when we came back to the pensione, Granny was dead. At first, we thought she was just mad about something, because she was sitting up stiff in her chair, staring straight ahead. But then we realized that she hadn't even opened her Pepsi. Dad shook her shoulder a little. "Verna? Verna?" he said, and then he turned to Mom and said, "Lizzy, she's dead." They hugged for a while, which made Jana so sick that she walked out of the room.

"How, how could she have—" poor Mom couldn't bring herself to say "died."

"I don't know, honey. She seems very peaceful, though."

"She does," said Mom, looking at Granny. "She looks happier than I've seen her for a while. Oh Hal, what if she was sick this whole time and I just thought she was being difficult?"

Dad thought for a minute. "Lizzy, I have to say that if Verna had been sick, I feel sure we would have known about it."

"You're probably right." Mom admitted.

Well, during all this I was staring at Granny, because I'd never seen a dead person before (except for those shriveled saints). She definitely looked dead. It's funny how different you look being dead. I'd always thought that you'd just look like you were asleep, but it's a whole different look. Less restful. Then I felt guilty because I wasn't having mournful thoughts about Granny. I tried to remember some times when we had had fun, but I couldn't really think of any except the time we went to the water slide, which was fun until I threw up and Granny said she was never going to take me anywhere again. Maybe she and Jana had had a better relationship.

By the time I stopped trying to have mournful thoughts, Mom and Dad were discussing what to do next. Dad went down to see Mr. Toffinelli, who ran the pensione, and after a few moments, Mr. Toffinelli came bustling into the room.

"Ahhhh," he said, looking at Granny. "Not sick. Dead. Many many sympathies, Signora. I feel your sorrow in my heart."

But then he got all efficient. Granny would have to be taken to the Magistrato in Perugia. There was no place in Assisi that did business with dead people.

"How do we get her from here to Perugia?" Mom asked. "An ambulance?"

No, no, no, he said. Ambulances were for sick people. Granny, he said, was not sick; she was dead.

"So what do we do?"

Well, it turned out what we had to do was put Granny in our car, dead, and drive up to Perugia ourselves.

"Isn't there a hearse?" cried Mom. Mr. Toffinelli looked baffled. Unfortunately, our diction-ary didn't contain the word hearse. I guess it doesn't come up that much.

"Is this what you do when someone dies?" Dad asked. Mr. Toffinelli said yes, certainly.

I think we were having communication problems.

After Mr. Toffinelli left, Dad tried to call the American Embassy in Rome, but all the lines were busy. "I'll try again tomorrow," he said. But the next day, the lines were still busy, and Granny wasn't looking so good. Since it was the middle of July, she wasn't smelling very good either. So Dad got directions to the Magistrato from Mr. Toffinelli.

I was afraid that Dad was going to ask me to help him put Granny in the car, so I made myself scarce after breakfast. After about an hour, I reappeared in the lobby.

"Where have you been?" Mom sounded pretty pissed.

"Bathroom." I tried to look pathetic.

"Humph. Go and get in the car."

I didn't want to sit next to a dead person, but I went outside. I almost laughed when I saw it. There was Dad at the wheel and Jana in the back seat with her head in her hands. Granny was tied to the top of the car. She was wrapped up in a sheet, very tastefully, so you couldn't tell it was a corpse. She looked kind of like a surfboard, actually.

Well, we drove and drove. All the stuff that looks close on the map is really far apart.

We finally got to Perugia around 2:30. It's one of those cities on the top of a hill, so everyone's driving like a maniac around and around this narrow road. Then they go skidding through the city and tear down a different road to get out. Dad was trying to find the Magistrato, but all the streets are one way, and nobody stops at the lights, so he was having a hard time. He had sweat on his upper lip.

After about a billion broiling hours, we found the right building, labeled Magistrato Inquirente, and trooped in, leaving Granny where she was for the moment.

Then things got really confusing. The guy at the desk couldn't understand us, so he got some other guy who was supposed to be practically English, but turned out not to be. After we finally got them to understand that Granny was a dead American, they told us to go to the Embassy, and Mom started to cry, saying we couldn't leave her tied to the top of the car for a whole trip to Rome. That was the point when they seemed to realize that we had a genuine dead person attached to our car.

"Perche no carro?" said Official Number 2. This turned out to mean "How come you don't have a hearse?" But thank God Mom didn't understand that until later.

Then they called out Official Number 3, who seemed to be a bigger deal than they were. They explained the situation to them, and we could tell when they got to the part about Granny being actually dead on the car, because Number 3 turned around to look at us with an expression of complete horror. "No!" he yelled.

"Si, si," they answered. We felt really stupid.

Then Number 3 got on the phone and explained the whole situation to someone else. At least, that's what we thought he was doing. He could have been ordering pizza for all we knew.

"Signora," he said after he hung up the phone, "We are necessary to bring your sad lose to the deposito, I think you call it mork."

"Yes! That's exactly what we want!" said Mom.

So then we waited a little while longer. Jana was flapping her eyelashes at Official Number 1 and Mom and Dad were just sitting quietly, holding hands. Then two guys come in with a big stretcher, and all of us—Mom, Dad, Jana, Officials Number 1, 2, and 3, the two stretcher guys, and me—went downstairs. We walked down a long hall and went through the fancy doors to the street. Dad stopped. The stretcher guys were standing respectfully behind him, waiting to have Granny pointed out to them. Dad looked to the left. He looked to the right. I was beginning to wonder what the problem was when I realized that our car was missing. The car and Granny—gone. For almost a minute, we all just looked up and down the street.

"Where'd she go?" Mom whispered.

Dad was looking at the parking space. There was broken glass on the ground. "They stole it," he said. "They stole the car."

"With Granny?" said Jana in a squeaky voice.

"I guess they didn't know it was Granny," Dad said slowly.

"I wonder if they know now," I said.

Mom made a gurgling sound in her throat, and Dad put his arm around her, but she was laughing, not crying. She laughed and laughed and laughed. We all started laughing. The officials looked at us. "Gli Americani," they said and went inside.

We drove back to Assisi and packed our bags. The next day, we went to Todi, which was very nice.

FAmOUs cheese of Poznan

Once upon a time lived a man named Grigory Pogojieff who thought that America was going to the dogs. "To the *dogs*," he emphasized. The causes of this sorry decline were various; sometimes Grigory laid the blame on the irradiation of produce; sometimes he felt that the low quality of television was responsible; sometimes he said it was that damned Jimmy Carter; but the single most important and oft-cited reason why Grigory felt the country was going to the dogs was disobedient children.

"Look at them!" he would yelp, waving his fingers at imaginary disobedient children in his living room, "They're rude, they sulk, they say bad words to their papas, they got no sense of responsibility, they're lazy, and they're stupid. They don't work, not lifting a finger, but they take, take, take the money that their papas make! This is terrible! This is why the country is going to the dogs!" Here, Grigory would turn to his own personal children and shake his fist, "If one of you ever says a bad word to me, I'll pound you. You don't do your homework, I'll pound you. You sulk, I'll pound you!"

They sat in a row—Alex, Avery, Annabel, and Armand—looking unimpressed. It must be said that Grigory rarely pounded any of them. But still, you never knew, so they pretended to be listening. Their jaws grew slack and their eyes clouded over. Now Grigory was on to the Von Trapp family. He just loved them.

"His word was law! He blows his whistle—TWEEE—and his children pour down the stairs! Discipline! It is the key for success for the Von Trapp family," Grigory turned an imaginary key. "And then, they sing, all together, beautiful!" He glanced sharply at his children. Avery had a little bit of drool falling out the side of her mouth. "Stop that!" he commanded. "Sing! All together, sing!"

"Sing what?" said Annabel suspiciously.

"Sing a beautiful song to make me happy. To warm my heart."

"Happy birthday to youuuu, happy birthday dear paaaaaapa, happy birthday to youuuuu," the children yelled.

Grigory clapped his hands over his ears and moaned in Polish. The children sighed and left the room one after another, and when Grigory stopped moaning and opened his eyes, all of them were gone.

The very next day, a mysterious package arrived at the Pogojieff house. It was lying on the doorstep when the children came home from school. Alex merely stepped over it, and Avery looked at it only long enough to determine that it wasn't her Lazy Daisy Super Stretch Denims For Only $44.95, but Annabel and Armand kneeled down together and inspected the package thoroughly, because, as Armand said, "it could be an explosive device."

It did not seem to be an explosive device. It smelled.

"Like when you leave lettuce in the vegetable drawer for too long and it rots and you don't know it and then you reach your hand in to find something to eat—like a pickle—and you touch this soft lump and then you think—"

"Shut up, Armand," said Annabel sharply. She stared at the small, square box. "This is trouble."

When Grigory—to whom the package was addressed—got home and opened it, he was at first in a quandary. "Who has sent me this box of dirt?" he roared. But, as he stirred the contents of the box with his finger he discovered that it was slightly sticky and very smelly and generally un-dirt-like. Suddenly, with a rush of joy, it came to him: this was the famous cheese of Poznan.

Now, the famous cheese of Poznan was of signal importance to all Poznanians, as it was the town's one contribution to the illustrious gastronomical tradition of Poland, but it was of particular importance to Grigory, whose few and precious memories of his early years in Poland were dappled with the famous cheese of Poznan. How his mother used to toss a bit of the famous cheese into his morning omelette or lightly dust a sausage with it! A keen emotion gripped his heart when he thought of her standing in her light-bathed kitchen, sprinkling the pale grayish-yellow flakes hither and yon (the famous cheese, I rush to mention, was usually eaten in a grated state as it was rather hard). As Grigory stood in his foyer, clutching the pungent gift to his bosom, a tear came to his eye. Who sent him this beautiful gift? He examined the painted box that housed the cheese, such a lovely tradition-al design. He searched through the wrapping, but found no card, no letter. Eagerly, he inspected the outer package. Ahh, the Chynosteka Street Pogojieffs, God bless them. Probably old Karol Pogojieff, remembering his favorite nephew. Grigory resolved to send the Chynosteka Street Pogojieffs a nice packet of peanut butter at his earliest convenience.

But now, there were omelettes to be made! Grigory strode briskly into the kitchen, gleefully envisioning his children's delight as they savored each bite of fluffy omelette harboring the famous cheese of Poznan.

Oh, what a flurry in the kitchen! Grigory dropped an egg in his excitement, and the cheese seemed lumpier than that of yesteryear, but soon, five gleaming omelettes lay on the respective plates of Alex, Avery, Annabel, Armand, and Grigory.

The children glanced at each other. They stared at the omelettes. Grigory beamed proudly at one and all. "Dig up," he said, lifting his fork.

Ah, the famous cheese of Poznan! But, strangely, the famous cheese did not taste as he remem-bered it. Grigory took another bite. Greasier. Sallower. Saltier. Age! thought Grigory. Age blights the memories of youth! What is delight for the young is greasy and bad for the old. My youth is gone, and I am dying. His sad reverie was interrupted by the realization that his children—vultures battening on his dying corpse—were not eating their omelettes. "Eat!" he commanded, "This is the famous cheese of Poznan!"

"It smells," said Annabel.

"Bad," said Avery.

"Like socks," said Alex.

"More like when you leave lettuce in the—"

"Shut up, Armand," said Annabel.

There was a long moment while Grigory looked at his offspring with amazed incomprehension. He lifted his hand slowly and smote his brow. "Aaaaach!" he bellowed. "God has given me ungrateful and disobedient children! They have betrayed not just their papa but their heritage, their stock, their people that they came from!" He smote his brow continuously during this speech. His face grew purple. "DIS-obedient children! If I said so much to my papa, do you know what happened to me? Slowly, off comes the belt, slowly he comes to me, looking hard in my eyes—" WHAP! Grigory slammed his fist on the table. "Children are begging for the tiniest taste of this cheese. In the streets! When I was a boy, all I wanted was this cheese of Poznan—for breakfast, lunch, and dinner. And you!—"

Avery picked up her fork and stuffed an enormous wad of omelette into her mouth. She gagged a little, but she got it down.

Alex sighed and did the same.

Annabel cast a furious look at her father and took a tiny bite.

Armand swallowed. "It's not bad," he said, his eyes watering.

Slowly with long pauses between bites, they finished their omelettes. Just as the last speck was consumed under Grigory's watchful eyes, Franny Pogojieff came home from work. As usual, she slammed the door energetically behind her. "I don't see why—" she began talking in the foyer, "I am the only one around here who can be bothered to look in the mailbox." Then there was a long silence. "Avery, something called Lazy Doozy Denims are on backorder. Armand, here is"—she entered the kitchen—"a sample issue of a magazine called Home Weaponry, which you'd better not have subscribed to. And Grigory, darling"—she leaned down to give him a hug—"we have some sad news from Eva. Uncle Karol is dead." Franny looked at the letter she held in her hands. "She says he had been sick all winter with bronchitis, but the doctor wouldn't let him come to the hospital because they didn't have enough beds, and then last month it turned into pneumonia. I'm sorry, dear." She patted Grigory's head sympathetically. Tears were streaming down his cheeks. "She says here that he always wished he could come to America like you did and so she's sent his ashes to be buried here. In a free land, she says, where the individual can triumph—HA!—but it's a nice sentiment. I guess we should have a little ceremony, take some pictures to send to—"

"—Mom!" said Armand urgently, "did she say when she sent those ashes?"

"What? Oh, um, she says that she sent them 'yesterday,' so that would make it, umm, about three weeks ago." Franny handed Grigory a tissue. "Did you all have dinner already? Anything left for me?"

Armand pushed back his chair and walked resolutely to the bathroom. They could hear him throwing up. Annabel and Avery figured it out at the same moment, and they didn't bother going to the bathroom. They threw up right at the table. Alex looked at them and ran out the back door. Franny stood frozen, her arms at her sides and her mouth open in a small O of alarm.

Grigory stopped crying and looked across the room at the jar containing what was left of Uncle Karol's ashes. For a minute, he felt a gentle relief that the famous cheese of Poznan could continue its hallowed existence in his memory, untrammeled by the incursions of reality. Then he, too, threw up.

Good
doG

In ORder to protect the identities of the people involved, who are under-standably quite embarrassed about their part in this drama, we have, with the help of noted animal psychologist Dr. Eben Rheingold, constructed the following episode from the point of view of the chief nonhuman character.

They stood out, that's for sure. Four blondes walking through the streets of Ankara, Turkey—you just don't see that every day. I told Olaf, "Heads up, dude, here comes dinner," but Olaf was chicken. Olaf liked to scrounge around in dirty corners, but not me. I was made for better things.

I could tell right away that they were Americans. I mean, they could have been Swedes, with that hair, but there was something about them that screamed AMERICANS! The way they walked, maybe. Confident, one foot in front of the other, no sly looks to the left or right, no hunched shoulders. Never a second's suspicion that someone was about to toss a bomb their way or that a policeman was just around the corner waiting to arrest them. Some of my friends found them intim-idating and some thought they were stupid, but when I saw Americans, I thought that's the place for me. It had to be better than stinking Ankara. If I could have been sure of ending up in the right country, I would have hitched a truck to Istanbul years ago. But unfortunately, Turkey's principal trading partner is Iraq.

Okay, so, these four Americans, they're walking right toward the Ankara Continental Hotel, which I happen to be intimately acquainted with, particularly the basement. I said to myself, Franz, get your butt over to the side steps in double time, and sure enough, that's where they came, marching up the stairs. Now I am no fool, and I knew better than to unveil myself to them immedi-ately, but I watched them. I wanted to get to know them, a father, a mother, a boy around eight, and a girl around ten. I figured that the girl was the key, and, as it turned out, I was right. The very next morning, around ten, the girl and boy came spiraling out of the lobby and down my stairs. Conventional wisdom would have been to skulk away into the shadows at that point, but I had a dif-ferent plan. I began to run down the stairs behind them, hopping along in a playful way. The girl noticed first, of course, and turned around to look at me. I have to tell you, I have a very appealing look—long glossy fur; a pointed muzzle; large, well-defined ears; and long legs—and I had already decided that I had to go for broke, so what I did was this: I stood up on my hind legs and begged.

Talk about instant success.

"Look at that cute little doggie! Davey! Look!" She was transfixed by me.

"Here pup, pup, pup," said the boy. I didn't move.

"He must be hungry, Davey. He's begging! Do you have any food?"

"I got a roll."

"Give it to him."

"What if I get hungry?"

"You can buy another roll. Give yours to the dog."

The boy pulled a nice plump wad of bread out of his pocket and held it out to me. For that, I would move. Very slowly, I approached him. He tossed it gently into the air and I caught it in my mouth.

"Wow!" they exclaimed, "He can do tricks! Let's go get a ball!"

A ball? What good is a ball? You can't eat a ball. But they thundered off. At this delicate moment, Kamer appeared. Now Kamer is a decent person, a sympathetic soul, truly, but his job is ridding the Continental of my ilk. He's much nicer about this than some people I could name who try to run us over with motor scooters. Kamer just said, "Go away. Shoo. Go home."

If only I could.

So I made myself scarce until the next morning, when the kids reappeared, dragging their mother along. The girl began jumping up and down when she saw me. "Look! Lookie, Mom, there he is! Here pup, catch a roll!" she squealed, tossing me another delicious lump of bread.

I caught it easily, and the mother laughed. "He's a circus dog, Sally. What a good boy! What's your name, boy?" she asked, kneeling down next to me and holding out her hand. I just looked plaintive. "Oh, you're a hungry doggie, aren't you?" she said, taking another roll from her pocket. She held it out to me, and exercising great self-control, I gently lifted it from her hand. Then I whimpered a little bit. That was the final straw for them. "Awww," they cried in unison.

After that, they were all over me. They'd bound down the steps to find me in the morning, and, in the afternoon, after seeing the sights, they'd stop by for a little visit. The boy began sneaking out after dinner, too, with tasty little snacks. The food got better each day; rolls gave way to pieces of omelette and pastries and thick meat pies, all delicious. I shared with Olaf and Pinky, but I have to admit, I got fat.

So, maybe a week went by, and one morning Sally says to me, "You are just so cute. I wish we could bring you home." Bingo.

By the afternoon, Sally and Davey and Mom are talking about it like it's a done deal. They'd clearly been doing some research, because they mentioned customs and dog carriers and Immigration and other official-sounding things. Even Dad comes out to take a look that evening.

"Well, he's not too big, at least. We'll see what we can do."

Two days later, Sally comes down the steps with a plastic cage. "Here pup, here pup," she says, holding out a meat pie like she's expecting me to run away. Ha! I got in that box so fast it made her head spin.

The trip—well, the trip was pretty bad. There was a passel of cats in the animal cargo, and they didn't like me one bit. One of them, a nasty gray thing with slitty green eyes, hissed and arched her back when she saw me. "You come near me and I'll bite your paws off, " I said and I meant it. Luckily, some jerk had decided to bring a marmot home, so the cats concentrated on terrorizing her and left me pretty much alone. It was freezing in there, too. I spent most of my time worrying about Customs. I was really sweating it, but the guy paid absolutely no attention to me or the family. He just waved us through. Americans have it good.

After that there was a lot of hugging and greeting of various people I presumed were relatives. I was displayed and admired and, more importantly, fed. Then, back in the cage, bump, bump, bump, and we're in the parking lot. I consider myself fairly cosmopolitan, but that parking lot took my breath away. Cars, hundreds of cars, stretching out as far as the eye could see. I hadn't known that there were that many cars in the whole world. It actually made me somewhat nervous; what if one of them broke loose, somehow? But my family was quite nonchalant about it, and I decided that, as their dog, I should be nonchalant too. Besides, there's something about being in America, something reassuring. In Ankara, one of the cars would break loose or crash into another car and people would run screaming through the streets, and someone would inevitably be mangled under the wheels, and the ambulance would get stuck in the market square for a half an hour, honking, and groups of people would stand around looking at the tragic accident and chatting about this and that. But in America, such things simply didn't happen. Cars behaved in an orderly fashion, and if they did crash into each other, no one was hurt, and if someone was hurt, the ambulance would instantly appear and whisk the victim away to a clean hospital, and bystanders would cluck sympathetically for a moment and then return to their duties.

We climbed aboard a gigantic car and drove to my family's home. It was a palace. Rooms galore, and I was allowed to investigate them all. The kitchen was my favorite, because it was just packed with food. And, get this, they left out bowls of food for me to eat, anytime I wanted. What a life. I slept on a soft blanket in a nice cozy basket, I got tons to eat, I was warm and dry and clean (they gave me baths). All they wanted in return was for me to catch a ball and go for walks with them. And not to poop in the house. They built a little door for me, so that I could go outside and poop whenever I needed to. They were very considerate, and I grew quite fond of them.

I knew it was too good to last. I knew it, but I was unprepared for what happened. It all began so innocently. One morning at breakfast, Mom said, "Charles, I'm going to take Cody to the vet this morning." They called me Cody; I don't know why.

"Okay," said Dad behind his paper.

"For what?" asks Sally.

"Distemper shots and stuff."

Distemper shots—that didn't sound good, but like I said, I had complete confidence in my family. I was sure they knew what was best for me. After we had done our morning puttering, Mom packed me into that same plastic cage and hauled me out to the car. We drove for a while and then she hauled me out and carried me into an office. It smelled terrible in there, like cats, but Mom didn't seem to notice. Finally, our name was called and Mom bumps me into a cold white room. There's a man in a white coat there, and he and Mom are exchanging pleasantries. She's telling him how they found me: " . . . on the steps of the hotel, and there he was, just the cutest little thing. He put up his little paws and begged and I'll tell you, from that moment on, we were goners."

"Mmm," said the guy in the white coat. He wasn't much interested in Mom's story, the boor. "Could you remove him from the carrier, please?"

"Come, Cody. Come on out, " said Mom encouragingly.

I didn't have a good feeling about it, but I did what I was told. I stepped out onto the doctor's white-paper-covered table, and tried to look charming.

"HUNH!" the doctor grunted, leaping backwards about six feet.

"What?!" said Mom sharply, looking around.

"That!" said the doctor, pointing at me.

"What!?" Mom said again, looking up and down.

"That's the—that's the biggest rat I've ever seen," he whispered.

"EEEEE! Where? Where?" shrieked Mom.

"There! There! Your dog!"

"What about my dog!?"

"IT'S A RAT!"

Mom stopped and gave me a good long look. For a couple of seconds, she just looked at me. Then she began to scream, "EEEEEEE, EEEEEEEEEE,. EEEEEEEEEEEEEEE."

Just like I'd always heard, the problem with Americans is prejudice. Once she knew I was a rat, Mom couldn't see the essential me; she could only see RAT. She couldn't say to herself, "What an extraordinary rat!" All she could think was that I was a failed dog. She didn't reflect on the hours of pleasure I had given her and the kids, all the fetching and playing I had done. The whole past was wiped out the minute she found out about my rattiness. Americans are limited, terribly limited.

While I was reflecting on this, Mom ran out the door in a panic, with the cowardly doctor close on her heels. I quickly realized that this privacy would be short-lived; they would undoubtedly be back with sticks and heavy objects, if not worse. So I took advantage of the open door and sidled out. I did not head for the front door—rats never go through the front door—rather, I nosed around for an open window, and finally found one, in a supply room. I could hear the sounds of frenzy around me, the screams and thuds of people looking for me, so I took the chance and threw myself out. Luckily, it wasn't a long drop, only six feet or so, and I landed in an extremely soft bit of grass. Physically, I was fine, but inside, I was heartsick. I had grown attached to my family, their sweet, silly ways and their affectionate natures. All that was over now. I hunkered down in the landscape, thinking about my future.

Ultimately, I decided to look on the bright side. I was in the land of opportunity, flowing with hamburgers and french fries and big Dumpsters, and although it was sad to give up my elevated and sanitary lifestyle, my new situation would have the advantage of allowing me to meet other rats. For I had decided never to stoop to deception again. I vowed to celebrate my rattiness, to luxuriate in my ratty qualities, and to develop my talents to their fullest. With this in mind, I set out to find a mall.

LigHt
beer

"Thanks, Sal. This is Eric Erlast, reporting from the scene of devastation that was downtown San Francisco. The conflagration has spread throughout the trendy South of Market neighborhood bordered by Fifth and Folsom streets, bringing specters of the Fire of 1906 to the eyes of terrified residents."

"Eric, this is Sal. Can you hear me?"

"Yes, I think I can, Sal."

"Eric, can you locate the source of this situation? Has the fire marshal made any sort of announcement or even guess as to the source?"

"Well, Sal, the rumors are flying here at the corner of Fifth and Folsom, but official reports have begun to come, and as they say, truth is stranger than fiction."

"That it is, Eric, that it is."

"Yes, Sal. [crash] Oh-oh. There goes the roof of the neighborhood's only parking garage. [moans] The crowd is gripped with despair, gripped with despair. I see one woman tearing her hair. It's a tragic scene, not unlike a battle—"

"Eric, you were going to pinpoint the origins of the fire for our viewers."

"Thanks, Sal, I was just trying to give a sense of the situation as it's being played out here. Official reports have located the fire's origins at the Lounge D'Or, that's the Lounge D'Or, at approximately 4th and Natoma, in the heart of trendy South of Market. The Lounge D'Or, one of the city's most popular karaoke sing-along bars, is now, of course, completely destroyed, and its entire clientele of some thirty persons is believed to have perished in the original fireball."

"Eric, this is a human tragedy of stunning proportions—"

"That it is, that it is—"

"Eric, has there been any speculation about the fireball? How could such a massive explosion occur?"

"Well, Sal, it's nearly unbelievable, but truth is stranger than fiction. Fire Marshal Arbuckle has announced that preliminary evidence indicates that the source of the flames is the new hydrogen beer recently imported from Japan."

"Hydrogen beer, Eric?"

"That's right, Sal. Hydrogen beer. According to Fire Marshall Arbuckle, hydrogen is used in place of the carbon dioxide in the brewing of Akira brand beer. Originally developed for environmental reasons, hydrogen beer has become a craze at karaoke bars due to its physical side effects. Like helium, hydrogen gas is lighter than air, which permits sound waves to be transmitted more rapidly. Sal, the result is that people whose lungs are filled with hydrogen gas can speak—and sing—in a high voice. The trendiest bars around the city, such as the Lounge D'Or, are sponsoring male soprano contests. Participants take a big gulp of Akira and see who can sing the highest note."

"Amazing Eric, but how does this relate to the devastating conflagration now raging in downtown San Francisco?"

"Well, Sal, hydrogen gas is highly flammable, and, according to reputable eyewitnesses, this has given rise to a new fad: After several gulps of Akira, your breath can be ignited with a cigarette, giving the impression that you are breathing flames. This is the so-called Dragon Effect."

"Unbelievable, Eric."

"Sal, I have here Dave Tanabe, who has actually seen this kind of activity performed. Dave, what can you tell us about the so-called Dragon Effect of hydrogen beer?"

"Uh. It's cool. It, um, looks good. You know, cool."

"But clearly the Dragon Effect has a dangerous side."

"No way, man. The guy was stupid."

"Which guy, Dave?"

"Joe Retzel, the guy who started all this. The guy at the Lounge D'Or."

"Are you saying that you know who precipitated this conflagration?"

"Yeah, Joe Retzel. He's an asshole."

"We're on television here, Dave."

"Oh. Sorry. He's a dweeb."

"Sal, it looks like we have access to the whole story here."

"Go ahead, Eric, we're with you."

"Tell me what happened, Dave."

"He was always trying to do this stupid thing. You know, you're supposed

to take like two swallows of beer, wait a second, and then take a drag on your cigarette, and breathe out, fast. Retzel thought it'd be really cool if he could light a
belch on fire, so he'd pound like four Akiras in a row, and then burp, but he's like
so stupid he could never get them lit up. Stupid white guy."

"You're saying the alleged perpetrator of the conflagration was trying to
set his burp on fire?"

"Yeah. No. No, see this time, he got it. See, I was outside the lounge, waiting for my girlfriend, and Barley, the bouncer, said that it was crowded because
Retzel was trying to light his burp. I mean, usually there's nobody there. I could
hear people cheering and then booing and stuff, and I was sort of pissed cause
my girlfriend was late, so I decided to bail on her and go to Zincaperm when I
heard this cheer—yay! and I thought oh, Retzel finally did it, and then there was
this scream. Loud and long. Barley opened the door to look inside and that's when
I saw Keiji Harlow. He was, like, in flames. It was gross. I was just thinking to
myself, Retzel burped too much, and then there was this big explosion. I hit the
ground, man, but Barley went flying. I heard him crashing onto the cars across the
street. I didn't want to look, man, so I just kept my head down. I could hear more
explosions and then sirens and then I ran—"

"So you're saying, correct me if I'm wrong, Dave, that this massive catas-
trophe was created by hydrogen beer."

"No, man, aren't you listening? It was created by Joe Retzel. What an a—
jerk."

"I'm stunned, Sal. This is astonishing. Whoops, there goes the venerable
Chronicle Building, the historic home of the San Francisco Chronicle."

"The irony of it, Eric. The irony."

"That's not the Chronicle Building, that's the Western Wool Coat Outlet."

"Thank you, Dave Tanabe, eyewitness to the remarkable and tragic origins
of this catastrophic fire."

"And that's Eric Erlast, reporting from downtown San Francisco, currently
in flames. Remarkable."

"Thanks, Sal."

"A Fresno woman with seven hundred shoes! More after this."

Telephone!

"**It'd kill her,**" said Clay.

"Aw, it wouldn't kill her. Women are tough," said Marcus.

"You don't know Nina. I gotta say, she's nuts about me. I mean, heh, it gets a little weird sometimes, how nuts she is."

"Like what? Jealous?"

"Oh. Well. Yeah. I mean, I think she suspects something's up, because when I come home late, Nina's in the living room, in the dark. It spooks me. I'll be all coming in, taking off my tie, trying to be quiet so I don't wake her up and all of a sudden I'll hear her voice saying, 'Clay's back,' and she's sitting there on the couch in the dark."

"And she pitches a fit?"

"Well. No. She just says something like 'Hard day at the office?' And I say yeah—oh wait, hold on," Clay's cell-phone was ringing, "Yeah, Clay. Hi. Yeah. No. Tell them to go fuck themselves. Okay. Look, we bought a full page and it better be a right-hand read. Call Rich and tell him that it's his ass if we don't get a right-hand. I don't care. Yeah." He clicked the phone off. "So I'm like yeah, real hard day, sorry I didn't call, didn't have a minute, whatever, and the whole time I'm thinking, is she going to smell Diane's perfume? Do I have lipstick on my shirt or whatever?"

"So then what does she say?" asked Marcus.

"Well, you gotta know Nina. She talks kind of bizarre. She says something like, 'I was just embroidering your monogram on your underwear.' "

"What?"

"You gotta know Nina. It's a kind of joke. I guess. You know, because you can't embroider in the dark? It's a joke. But she's like totally crazy about me. Totally."

"So why're you going to dump her?"

"Like on Sunday, right? She was wearing this little bathrobe thing I got her, and I kind of patted her on the ass when she was walking by, and she jumped my bones, man. It was great."

"Why—"

"Oh wait, dude. Sorry. I've gotta make a call. I forgot. I gotta call Sherman." Clay fingered his phone and punched out some numbers. "Oh. wait. He's on my speed dial. Wait. What's his code? I wrote it down someplace." He rifled through his wallet until he found a carefully trimmed index card. "Here. Okay." He punched two numbers. "Shermie, dude! Howzit goin'? Yeah. I hear you. I hear you. What's going on on Saturday, dude? Oh. I thought you said you were going to the game. The Giants, dude! Oh. Okay. Okay. Later, dude." Clay turned to Marcus. "Sorry. What did you say before?"

"I said why are you going to dump her if she's so hot?"

"I'm not sure I'm going to dump her, man. But, like, Diane, she's a partier. She's up for anything, you name it. And it's kind of cool that we've got the same job, you know, so we have stuff to talk about. I mean, Nina, she's like reading books and going to museums, and, like, she tried to get me to go to the fucking opera. I was all no way. Diane's more normal. You could go to a ball game with Diane."

"Nina won't go to the game? Loser." Marcus stuck his finger in his drink and whirled it around.

"Oh, she'll go. But, like, we went to a game last week or whatever, and she's sitting there reading The New Yorker. Which really got on my nerves after a while because, I mean, she's at the fucking game! So it was like the sixth inning, and I'm pissed and I tell her to put the damn magazine away and watch the game," said Clay aggrievedly.

"She wouldn't, huh?"

"No. No, that's not it. She did. And she got totally into it, the game I mean. Staring like crazy, watching every move. So at the end, I say something like aren't you glad I told you to put the magazine away? And she says, get this, she says, 'Yeah, it's like a Brueghel.' "

"A what?"

"Fuck if I know, dude. But it kind of ruined the game for me. Diane wouldn't say shit like that."

"Yeah," Marcus nodded.

"But she's a babe. Nina, I mean. Oh. I should call her. So she doesn't worry and stuff." Clay withdrew his cellphone from its pouch and concentrated on its buttons. "Hiya, Nina. Me. I'm going to be kind of late, babe. Like midnight. Yeah. Don't wait up. You are? Where? Have I been there? Well. Have a good time? Take a taxi, okay? Yeah. Bye."

"I always say make it short and sweet, bro. Just tell her it's over and you want her out."

"Brutal, man," said Clay.

"Otherwise, it's like you gotta go out to dinner and talk about your relationship and then she cries at the table and everyone looks at you like you're a big asshole. It sucks. That's what happened with Karen. So I, like, learned my lesson, and when I wanted to break up with Margaret, I just said, 'Sorry, sweetheart, it's been fun, but it's over.' "

"And then—what?—here's your suitcase? Whoa."

"No, it wasn't that bad, I swear. I was like, 'I hope you can leave by this weekend, because I'm going to repaint the walls.' Or something like that. And she was, like, outta there the next day."

"And she was, like, okay?"

"I guess so," Marcus shrugged.

"Wow. That's wild." Clay thought for a minute. "Oh, shit. I gotta call the office." He pulled out his phone. "Marcy. Put Jack on, okay. Yeah. Jack! We gotta get out the plans for Dustup tomorrow. Yeah. No. They called me today, all pissed. They wanna see it now. That's what I told them. Yeah. Well, that's what they said. Stegenberger's going to kill us if we lose them. Yeah. Okay. We can do it in the morning. Like six. Okay. Take it easy, Jack-man. Okay." He clicked the telephone off. "What a hard-ass. He's all, if Dustup's going out tomorrow, why aren't you in the office tonight? Cause I, like, have a life, man. Asshole. I gotta get there at six tomorrow. Shit."

Marcus nodded sympathetically. "Assholes."

"I guess I should go." Clay got to his feet. "Gimme the bill here, bro," he said to the bartender.

Same bar, seven weeks later.

"It's all your fault, man," Clay was saying. "You should pay the damn bill."

"Hey. Chill, dude. What's the deal?" Marcus was mixing his drink with his finger again.

"Remember? Last time we're here, you're all telling me 'Break up with Nina, just give her the boot and show her the door.' You said make it short and sweet, no muss, no fuss, right?"

"I guess so, man. Didn't work out?"

"So a couple days later, Stegenberger says I gotta go to Jakarta for this new account, InterBank whatever. Gotta go for two weeks. And I'm thinking, two weeks, this is the perfect thing. I'll tell Nina that it's over and then I'll give her, like, two weeks. I'll say she just has to be gone when I get back, right?"

"Yeah?"

"That, like, seemed nice, compared to you," said Clay.

"Fuck you, dude."

"Right. Just lemme tell you what happened. So I go home, it was like a Friday, and I'm flying out the next day. You know, I bring home roses and everything—"

"Why're you bringing her roses if you're breaking up with her, dude?'

"Well. I just did. I don't know. So I'm all calm and I'm saying, like, I don't think this is working out and I'm not ready for commitment and all like that, and she's just staring at me. And then I kind of run out of things to say and she's just looking at me. Doesn't say anything. So finally, I'm all 'What? What's up with you?' And she says, 'I'm waiting for your phone to ring.' She was always on about the phone, how it's like this total waste of time, whatever. Anyway, so I say that I gotta go to Jakarta for two weeks and I expect her to be gone when I come back. And, dude, it, like, came out all wrong. She looked at me like I was a sack of shit. Man, that sucked." Clay fell silent for a moment. "Then she said, 'I see. May I be permitted to pack my possessions, or would you like to simply throw them out the window?' "

"She talks like that?"

"Yeah. Yeah. You gotta know Nina. I kind of liked that about her. Even though it was a pain in the ass sometimes. You know?"

"Sort of."

"So I'm all 'You can pack, sorry,' but she doesn't say anything. Nada. Not a word. After a couple hours, I couldn't take the tension, so I went to a bar. I actually kind of stayed out all night. Came back around like five in the morning to get my suitcase and my plane ticket, and all of Nina's stuff was stacked up in boxes. All the books and these pictures of fruit that I kind of liked and this stupid quilt she was totally crazy about, stacked up neat in a corner. Nina was asleep on the couch, which made me feel like a sack of shit again, like she couldn't even sleep in the bed or something. So I tiptoe around, trying to pack my suitcase in the dark. I didn't even take a shower because I was scared I'd wake her up. I was pretty rank by the time I got to Jakarta, man, pretty rank. Not like anyone noticed, though. What a dump."

"You didn't even say good-bye to her, man?" asked Marcus incredulously.

"Whaddaya mean? You're the one who said to make it short and sweet! I already felt like a sack of shit, and so what, I'm supposed to wake her up and she's either all sad and I feel like a dick or she's all mad and I feel like a dick. Gimme a break. Shit."

"I dunno, man. I would have said good-bye."

"Great, man, you're making me feel great," said Clay gloomily.

"So was she gone? When you got back?"

"Oh yeah. She was gone. Totally gone. But she left a message."

"What'd she say?"

"Remember what I was saying in the beginning? You should pay the bill? What Nina did was, she called for the time in Kyoto; you know, the phone number where they tell you what time it is, they have that in Japan, too. So, Nina called that number and just left the phone there. For two weeks, while I was gone. A two-week phone call to Kyoto."

"Wow. That's fucked. Whoa. How much is it?"

"Eight thousand four hundred and eighty-nine dollars."

"That's totally fucked. Did you call the phone company? You know, to tell 'em what happened?" Marcus asked.

"Yeah."

"What'd they say?"

"The woman laughed. She said, 'You go, girl!' and that it wasn't the phone company's problem. Shit."

"Whoa. That's brutal. Can't you find her and make her pay?"

"Don't know where she is."

"Call her friends or something," suggested Marcus.

"I did. They told me to fuck off. They never liked me and now they hate me. Assholes. Her mother even told me to fuck off."

"Man, you're screwed. You should have said good-bye."

"I told you, stop saying that. Look," Clay fumbled in his wallet, "she left me this note, too. Take a look:

pity this busy monster, manunkind

not. Progress is a comfortable disease.

What the fuck does that mean? And then it says "e. e. cummings" underneath. With no capital letters, which is weird, cause Nina was into spelling."

Marcus angled his head to take a look. "Weird chick, man. I guess at least you're free."

"Yeah. Yeah. I guess."

"What? This is what you wanted, right?"

"Yeah. I guess."

"So you and Diane—huh?" Marcus leered questioningly.

"Oh. I didn't call her yet."

"What? I thought that was, like, the point!"

"Yeah. I've been busy, though."

"You are one weird dude."

"Yeah, I guess." Clay looked morosely at his drink.

the day
it Rained
in
Los Angeles

In 1983, all over the sunny hills and dales of Los Angeles, mothers were saying one of the following things:

1. You look like you've been poured into them!
2. Absolutely not!
3. Can you even sit?
4. No daughter of mine is going out of the house looking like that!

In reply, the daughters were saying one of these things:
1. Mother! God!
2. Everyone else is wearing them.
3. You're totally ruining my life!
4. They aren't even tight.

In some cases, the daughter prevailed; in some cases, the mother prevailed. Their respective victories were purely ideological, though, because the daughter who lost the battle would merely place her extremely tight jeans in her backpack, skulk into the school bathroom in her maternally approved garments, and emerge triumphantly bound into her pants.

How to describe these pants? Teenage girls all over the country were lying down on their pink and white beds, under the resentful eyes of their recently abandoned Barbie dolls, and slowly inching their jeans over their skin, pulling and holding their breath and pointing their toes. In Los Angeles, a town devoted to intimations of sexual abandon, the girls were more sophisticated and bought their jeans so tight that they had to dress in clusters, the wearee supine and three confrères pulling up the jeans. One would think that the bonds of friendship created in such a situation

would be indelible, but one would be wrong. Vertical, it was every girl for herself. Some handy (and limber) girls even restitched the legs of their pants once they were on, in order to make them tighter than was feasible for people with feet. This adjustment was called pegging and was the last word in style.

At Orange Grove High in West L.A., Nancy Silverlake was renowned for her thick brown hair, the fact that she had done it on a tennis court, and her tight pants. In a school famed for tight pants, hers were the very tightest. Walking stiffly through the halls, she laughed and screamed in the unvarying rhythms of high school girls, brushed soulfully against some boys and ignored most, and swung her hair in a fetching manner. Her pants were so extremely tight that she could not sit down in class. "I have a bad back," she explained to her teachers. "I gotta stand."

"Hmmmm," said all the girls wearing sensible pants.

"I do!" said Nancy.

Then, one unfathomable morning, it rained in Los Angeles and Nancy Silverlake died. Right there in Advanced Algebra, she turned red, and then white, and then blue. Mr. Crepisi, the teacher, whose reputation rested on his rumored addiction to Blistex, danced around Nancy's fallen figure ineffectually. An assortment of girls screamed, and one or two students ran to the office for help. By the time the paramedics arrived, it was too late, and they were relegated to brawnily carrying out the corpse.

It was an exciting lunch hour. The school was abuzz with the tale of Nancy Silverlake's demise, and clutches of teenagers stood about in the drizzle comparing rumors.

"I heard she was doing coke for seven days straight."

"She had reds. I saw."

"She was drunk all the time."

"That guy she was going with gave her heroin. He's in a gang."

"Maybe someone killed her."

"I heard her sister hated her."

But then Paulette Twigg fell to the floor of her fifth-period chemistry class. Red, then white, then blue, and out. Again, the paramedics trotted manfully to the scene; again, their duties consisted of merely toting the corpse. Then Theresa Listerman crashed to the linoleum of fifth-period French, evading dictation by death. Marlene Ramirez toppled over in sixth-period literature of California, breaking her nose and dying at the same moment. Mallory TerHont collapsed in seventh-period drama, but by this time, the school was crawling with paramedics, and she was saved.

"Pants," gasped Mallory. Bill and Bob, the paramedics, glanced at each other in consternation. Pants?

"Pants," she gasped more softly. They were losing her.

Hoyt Sanders, reviled since kindergarten as a brain, alternately spat on, teased, and ignored, his tenderest feelings held up to ridicule, his every action mocked, his days a miasma of humiliation and loneliness, spoke up. "Her pants. They're too tight. She can't breathe."

The paramedics, somehow catching the whiff of degradation that hung around Hoyt, snorted.

"Fine. She's going to die in about thirty seconds," Hoyt said. He didn't care.

"Bob?"

"Okay, okay." Bob reached out a cautious hand and unbuttoned the top button of Mallory's pants. She was beginning to turn blue.

"That's not going to do it, guys," said Hoyt. "It rained, right? She got wet and her pants shrunk and now her pants are pushing her intestinal tract into her lung cavity. You gotta take her pants off."

"You!" said Bob pleadingly.

"No way," said Hoyt grimly.

Together, Bob and Bill unzipped the unconscious Mallory's pants and began to peel them off. A cluster of boys and girls stood about in unabashed fascination, particularly when it turned out that Mallory didn't wear underwear. "Whooo," said one boy hysterically.

"Shut up, Dean," said everyone else.

Grunting, Bob and Bill tugged at her pants. They pulled. One or two helpful types yanked on the bottoms. Slowly, they released her belly and thighs from the captivity of her pants. Mallory turned white. Her eyelids fluttered. She came to, and found herself lying pantless in the center of a circle of admiring spectators. This was her dream. "Where am I?" she asked dramatically.

"Nowhere," said Hoyt Sanders.

Later, Dr. Ule Ogan, a gastroenterologist, confirmed Hoyt's diagnosis. The wet pants had shrunk, he said, pushing the girls' large and small intestines up into their stomachs, which, in turn, invaded their lung cavity. "These pants are a hazard," he said, holding up Mallory's shredded jeans.

"Not really," said Hoyt. "If you think of the big picture, these pants are terrific. Stupid girls buy them, get wet, and die. It clears the gene pool. Fewer stupid people reach the age of reproduction and so the human race gets smarter."

Dr. Ogan nodded admiringly and clapped Hoyt on the back. "Son," he said, "there's a new field called genetic engineering, and I think you ought to consider it."

While this conversation was taking place, Mallory TerHont was some miles away, at the Beverly Center, shopping for a new pair of pants.

Walk the dog

Once upon a time, Joe Veitz had to go out of town. It was an emergency, in fact. Joe was a structural support engineer, which meant that he built scaffolding, and, unfortunately, one of his scaffolds had collapsed. Kerplunk. Fell right to the ground. Even more unfortunately, at the moment of its collapse the mayor of Greenleesboro was standing on it, cutting a ribbon. He had been accompanied on the scaffolding by a variety of dignitaries, including Steve, Don, Ron, and Jon Dermato, the famous quadruplets of Greenleesboro. Even now, the staff of the Jeff Davis County coroner's office was struggling to reassemble Don, Steve, and Jon from their constituent parts. It didn't help that they were identical. At the first groan of metal, Ron had flung himself from the flimsy platform on which he stood, getting by with a mere concussion. It was funny, the people of Greenleesboro agreed, that Ron, of all the quadruplets, should be saved, since he was the one nobody liked. Oh, sure, some people had never forgiven Jon for biting Clarice's dog, but most chalked that up to boyish pranks. Well, anyway, it was just too bad. Good thing their mother hadn't lived to see the day.

But Joe Veitz had to leave home to visit the site of the tragedy in his official capacity. His boss, Sandro, made him go. "Listen, you, I want you standing there with tears in your eyes. You hear me? I want manly grief, and I want it where everyone can see it," Sandro said, twisting his neck against his collar. Sandro was a man who always looked as though he would be more comfortable in something other than what he had on.

"Aww, Sandro, I said I was sorry. I don't know what the hell happened up there. I did everything the way I always do it," said Joe.

"That's what I'm afraid of. I want a full report. I want to know where it fell apart first, I want to know how many people were on it, I want to know the order they fell in. Ohhhh," Sandro rocked back and forth, plucking at his tie, "the insurance guys are going to kill us."

"I know, Sandro, but couldn't I go tomorrow? I kind of got some stuff to take care of here." Joe was twitching in his vinyl chair. "I could leave tomorrow early."

"NO! You get on the plane this afternoon, you goddamn prick, and find out why your scaffold killed all those people whose relatives are going to sue my ass. TODAY! TODAY! TODAY!" Sandro was scarlet red.

"Gee, okay, okay. You don't have to get so mad. Okay. I'll go. I gotta call Cheryl, though."

"Call whoever you want," said Sandro into his hands.

Joe tiptoed back to his cubicle. He clutched at the telephone and pressed buttons furtively.

The theme song from *Jungle Book* twittered innocuously into his ear for thirty seconds. "Hi, it's Monique. Leave me a message and have a great day!"

A massive beep rattled Joe's tympanum. "Hi," he whispered hoarsely, "it's me. I got to—"

Another titanic beep erupted, and a sterile recording came on, "Incoming message tape full. Please try again."

Frantically, Joe dialed again and heard the recording again. He shouldn't have been surprised, because it happened every day. It was Monique's mother, Delores. She lived in Radio, Texas, and called at 10 a.m. each morning to give a report on the status of her garden. Sometimes there were snails, sometimes aphids, occasionally earwigs; the day her clematis bloomed, she described every hue and shimmer. Mulch, tomatoes, cucumber, and agapanthus. Roses, tea and floribunda, new and antique. Monique asked her to call in the evening, but Delores went to bed at 7 because, she explained, if you want to kill snails, you've got to get up at 4. Then Monique bought a one-minute message machine, but Delores simply called back until the tape ran out, and, since she forgot what she had already said, she repeated herself in an aggravating fashion. Then Monique tried calling Delores at 9 a.m., but that didn't stop Delores from calling at 10. Finally, Monique had bought a cell-phone. Joe was rapidly dialing the number. "I'm sorry, the party you are dialing is out of range," said a soothing telephonic voice. Joe slammed down the phone and cursed.

"Are you still here?" screamed Sandro from his office. "Get to the damn airport, Joe, before I give in to temptation and fire you."

"I got to stop off at the house and feed the dog," Joe said plaintively.

"Listen, you prick, there are twelve people dead at Greenleesboro. The dog can be hungry for a few hours. GO!" Joe could hear Sandro's shirt ripping.

Joe left.

As she stepped out the door of Sitting Pretty Chairs for All Occasions, Cheryl Veitz had an inspiration. Fondue. Only Thursday, she had been reading an article in *Country Kitchen*, all about the fondue renaissance. "Fondue's Back!" it was called, and it featured a photograph of a woman much like herself, smiling fondly at a beefy man who was in turn smiling fondly at a fondue pot. Cheryl had been reminded that she had received a fondue set for her wedding, a tasteful metal bowl accompanied by brightly colored fondue forks. If there was anything Cheryl felt strongly about, it was the importance of using wedding presents. She couldn't stand people who put away their wedding china and never used it. "My china makes every meal special," she often said at appropriate junctures, such as wedding showers. But she had never taken her fondue set out of the box, she reminded herself, not once. "Fondue's Back!" had included a tasty-looking recipe for cheese fondue. "Serve with a simple green salad, and sit back and watch your family enjoy their first fondue adventure!" the story had concluded. Well, she and Joe could have a fondue adventure tonight, thought Cheryl, for the price of a hunk of Swiss cheese and some Sterno. She recalled another Country Kitchen article, "Family Time Is Festive Time," all about how you should dress up for dinner and dot your end tables with simple bouquets from the garden, and she resolved that for their fondue adventure, she would wear her new pink ensemble, which Joe had seemed to like when she showed it to him. At least, he had nodded. "Nice," he had said.

As she turned into the parking lot of the supermarket, she allowed herself to wonder about Joe. Sometimes he seemed so absent-minded. She might even call it thoughtless, maybe. Like he would go to the store and she would say, Get a thing of cottage cheese, and then he would come back two hours later with teabags. I thought you said teabags, he would say, sorry. And take the new pink ensemble, for instance. He hadn't even really looked at it; he had just nodded. But then, he had a lot of worries, far more than she did. His job for instance. Sitting Pretty Chairs for All Occasions was much easier than scaffolding, she knew. Scaffolding was high pressure. All she did was tell people to come in and take a load off. Everyone liked to have a little rest, and once she got them off their feet, she would start talking about how practical peach upholstery was or something and before you knew it, they were shelling out $350. Easy.

By the time Cheryl stepped through her door, bearing Sterno and Swiss and almost stepping on the head of C3PO, their dog, Joe was fastening his seatbelt in preparation for landing at the Jeff Davis County airport, serving Snipesville, Pridgen, Lumber City, and Greenleesboro. By the time she had called out his name and received no answer, Joe was listening helplessly as the recording repeated for the fifth time, "I'm sorry, the party you dialed is out of range."

Finally Cheryl noticed that she had a message. "Hiya. Cheryl? It's me, Joe. I guess you're not home. Um. I'm not home either, but, uh, I guess you know that. What happened is, one of my scaffolds—the one down in Greenleesboro—it broke. Some people died, I guess, so Sandro said I had to come down to make a report and, you know, apologize. He said I had to go like right away and the line was busy at Sitting

Pretty, so I'm at the airport now. Sorry. But what I really wanted to say was I don't think you ought to take C3PO out for a walk tonight. I was thinking he seemed kind of sick this morning, so I think he shouldn't have a walk tonight. Okay? I mean, it would be bad if he got sicker or something. So, don't take him out for a walk, okay? Okay. I'll be back tomorrow. Probably tomorrow. Bye. Love you. Bye."

Cheryl slammed her Swiss onto the counter. What about her fondue, did he ever think of that? C3PO looked at her in alarm and whimpered, and suddenly she felt ashamed. Joe didn't even know about the fondue, of course. "We can have fondue any old time," she said to the dog. Poor Joe, with his collapsed scaffolding. Sandro was just plain mean, she thought. "Why should Joe have to go and apologize?" she whispered fiercely to C3PO, "Isn't it Sandro's company? Doesn't he make all the money? He should apologize himself, if he wants apologizing." She thought of Joe, all alone down in Greenleesboro, probably feeling just terrible about those people, who should have been more careful, she was certain.

C3PO whimpered again, looking at her earnestly. "Oh, Seepie, your dinner!" cried Cheryl. Even his water dish was dry. Cheryl rubbed his ears and busied herself with the water and dog food. "You sick, Seepie? Joe says you're sick, old Seepie-seepie. Maybe you were just having a premonition about that scaffolding." She glanced at him wonderingly. His eyes were fixed on his dish.

"Woof," he replied hopefully.

She set the dish down in front of him, and he dove toward it, his ears flapping with excitement. He gobbled it down in a frenzy of delight as Cheryl listlessly prepared a Swiss cheese and mayonnaise sandwich for herself. She took a bite and chewed mechanically as C3PO grunted and whuffled into his bowl. Her kitchen was nothing like the kitchens in *Country Kitchen*. It was brown, for one. And the curtains were all wrong. She needed curtains with little flowers on them. And maybe a matching banquette. Where would she put a banquette? she wondered. Joe could make her one; he was good with things like that. A little banquette with a table in front of it, next to the window. Cute.

"Woof," said C3PO again. He wanted more.

She leaned down and spooned out the rest of the can. He dove into his bowl once more, slurping and snorting. He didn't seem sick to her. He seemed hungry. Satiated, he lunged toward his water bowl, lapping madly. "Woof," he barked again, gratefully. What a dinner.

Cheryl reached down for his ears and rubbed them idly. "Good old Seepie. Guess you're feeling better, right? You a premonition dog? Premonition doggie-woggie?"

C3PO walked away, toenails clicking. Cheryl felt depressed. Even the dog had left her. Eat and run. May as well be a restaurant, she thought. The toenails clacked back toward her. It was C3PO, holding his leash in his mouth.

Cheryl laughed, "You're not sick, are you, Seepie? Want a walk? Want a walk, old boy? Come on." Feeling needed, she dropped her sandwich to its plate and stood up.

Within seconds, they were out the door.

In those same seconds, Monique Ferier was screeching her Miata to a halt in her little driveway. She flung open the car door and ran into her tiny bungalow. Joe was coming any minute, any minute, and she was covered with the smell of Reynold Shoate. Leaving her front door slightly ajar, Monique unbuttoned her slate gray business suit with trembling fingers. Reynold had ripped her blouse, getting it off. If Joe saw, she was in big trouble. Shower, shower, shower. Peeling off her hose and stuffing everything into the washing machine, Monique dashed toward the bathroom. She would say it was all for him. She would say, "I've got nothing on but my perfume, baby." There's no way he would notice a thing. She turned the hot water on as high as it would go, just as Cheryl and C3PO turned the corner of her street.

Cheryl was amazed. Every night after dinner, Joe took Seepie for a walk. Sometimes, when they were first married, she used to come along, but it had been over a year since she had walked the dog. He was so fast. She hadn't remembered that. He pulled her along briskly, turning from this street to that as though he had a map. She was surprised that Joe walked this fast for more than an hour every day; she knew she couldn't keep up the pace for that long. She was already breathless. C3PO was trotting ahead of her, his leash dangling behind, and—oh wait, he was on someone's lawn. Cheryl hurried on, hoping he wasn't going to pooh. "Seepie. Here, Seepie," she called softly, but he moved up the garden path toward the front door. "Seepie, come," Cheryl said, following him. Where in the world did he think he was going? The door seemed to be ajar, and the dog nudged it with his nose and pushed his way in. "Seepie! Come!" said Cheryl in the strangled voice of someone trying to scream in a whisper.

From inside the house, Cheryl heard a woman's voice: "Hi, C3. Go get your treat, boyo" and then the front door opened wide to expose a flood of light and a naked woman peering into the dark. "Joooooo-ey," she sang suggestively, "I've got nothing on but my perfume."

Cheryl stood, still as a statue, on the dark lawn. She thought, irrelevantly, about the fondue she had almost made. She thought of Joe eating her fondue and looking at the clock, waiting to take the dog for a walk and do whatever he did with this girl. She pictured leaning across the kitchen table and stabbing him with her sharp-pronged fondue fork, right in the chest. "You can just go to hell," she yelled toward the doorway. Then she went home, mildly comforted by the sound of C3PO following her, his leash dragging behind him.

Know Your Man

I could tell right then that they were going to do it. I've known Sean for ten years, and he had that look on his face. He just can't stop himself. He says it's because he loves women and wants to make them happy, but, as far as I can tell, by the time he's done with them, they're not as happy as they were before they met him. Here's how I knew they were going to do it: Sean was holding up his plate for seconds on the apple pie. He said, "They don't feed me at home," and he gave her that old smile of his.

Then Lila said, "Oh, honey, I can tell. You're thin as a sheet of paper," and she kind of poked him in the belly. Then they looked at each other for about twenty seconds without blinking.

I just kept working on my pie. It's like that being Sean's friend; sometimes you've just got to pretend you're somewhere else. I remember once in college, he and this girl did it in a study cube at the library. I was in the next cube, and all of a sudden, there's all this breathing and thumping and stuff, so I put my head around the edge of Sean's cube. I thought he was having a heart attack, I swear I did. And so there I am face to face with Sean's bare butt and this long leg with a pair of underpants wrapped around the ankle. So what's etiquette? Apologize for interrupting? I decided that I should just pretend it wasn't happening and get back to work, and that's what I've been doing ever since.

I have to say, I was surprised this time. I mean, when we were driving up her driveway, and she was standing on the porch, I thought, Wow, she's beautiful. But Lila was one of those women who looked a lot better from a distance than she did up close. It didn't have to be much of a distance, maybe two feet, but it made a big difference. At two feet, you got a general sense of big brown eyes, high cheekbones, a cloud of silvery-blond hair, and this very nice figure. At one foot, you noticed that cloud was pretty wispy and the high cheekbones were covered with makeup. But still, she had a nice look, and I bet twenty-five years ago she took no prisoners. See, Sean and I had been driving out from Portland, where we had done a big presentation. We thought we were going to get to State Bend by dark, but it was farther than we thought, and about 5:30 we saw this sign, "Grangier Farm Bed and Breakfast," so we pulled in. There was Lila, standing on the porch. She seemed pretty surprised to see us. "You saw the sign?" she said, "In the entire history of the Grangier Farm Bed and Breakfast, nobody has ever seen that sign. Sometimes I think I should just take it down and tell people that part of the fun is looking for the place. Not that there's so many people to tell. Well, come on in. You can have any room in the house."

It was a nice place, although a little lonely, and it had all those bed-and-breakfasty touches, like flowery pillows and little bitty soaps and potpourri. There was no one else there. "I'm the widow

Grangier," said Lila cheerily as she made dinner. We were sitting in the kitchen, sipping sherry. At least I was sipping sherry. Sean had asked if she had anything stronger, and Lila had produced a bottle of Wild Turkey. They were both drinking Wild Turkey. "The Grangier Farm Bed and Breakfast was supposed to give me a new interest in life after the death of my husband."

"Has it?" asked Sean.

She winked at him. "Intermittently."

That was when the flirting began. Wow, I thought, Sean has met his match. Pretty soon, every sentence was heavy with innuendo and significant glances were flying through the air. I just ate my Turkey Tetrazzini. Lila was a dynamite cook, and the wine was flowing. By the time we got to the apple pie, though, I was depressed. Being Sean's friend is hard on the ego; it's like you're not even there most of the time. I mean, when we're working together or hanging out together, it's cool. He's a funny guy, and we have a good time. But once there's a woman in the room—boom! I'm invisible. Like I said, I've know Sean ten years, and let me tell you, I've had just one girlfriend who didn't fall for him. Even the ones who said they hated him turned out to secretly dig him. Actually, now that I think about it, the ones who hated him were the ones who ended up sleeping with him while they were dating me. Most of the others took the high road: I don't think I can see you any more because I have feelings for Sean. So we'd break up, and Sean would call me a few days later saying "Hey Jim, man, Karen's calling me. Are you guys over? Can I go out with her?"

And I'd say go ahead.

Arianna. She was the one who didn't fall for Sean. When she met him, I watched her like a hawk. "So, what did you think of Sean?" I asked her.

"Which one was Sean? The big guy with the blue shirt? He seemed nice," she said. God, did I love her. I kept trying to find out why she wasn't attracted to him. At first, she would talk about it. "I don't like his muscles." "His nose is weird." But then she got fed up. She thought I was obsessed with Sean; when she broke up with me, she said she thought I was in love with him myself.

Anyway, after the thing about the apple pie and the poke in the stomach, I excused myself and went to bed. I woke up in the middle of the night and heard them laughing in the room next door.

●

That boy was a breath of fresh air, I'll tell you. Men my age are so tedious, fussing about their taxes and their prostates and checking the restaurant bill with a microscope practically. It wasn't always like that. Twenty-five years ago, men wanted to make me laugh; they were desperate to entertain me, to charm me, to somehow get me into their bedrooms. Not that I was easy. Especially after I was married, I was quite discriminating. A man had to have that flair, that special way of looking at me, before I'd even consider it, even after Thomas was in the wheelchair. Thomas, now, he was old, or I thought he was old back then, but he had flair. I just loved Thomas. He never talked to me about taxes or, God forbid, his prostate, and when it was time to leave the restaurant, he glanced at the bill and threw down a wad of cash and we swept out. They don't make them like him any more. But this boy, this James, he reminded me of Thomas. He understood the importance of the glance and of language. So many men think that it's all about pawing bodies. Idiots. James was one of those men who are simply born knowing how to please women, one of the few who doesn't see relations between men and women as a battlefield but as a bed—a soft, endless bed.

Of course, you can't expect a man like that to be monogamous. For most of my woman friends, this an insurmountable obstacle, but I find that kind of thinking to be parochial. The advantage is that this kind of man doesn't expect you to be monogamous either. Thomas, for instance, had affairs throughout our marriage, which didn't bother me a bit (with the exception of Meg Myerling, who lasted too long for my taste), and he didn't fuss too much when I did the same (with the exception of Stephen Walchester, who was my retaliation for Meg). I could tell that James had been around the block more than a few times, and this didn't bother me. In fact, I found it reassuring. I don't want to be some fool's teacher; I want to enjoy myself. Which I did, quite a lot, with James.

Of course, one doesn't want to feel the tramp, either. When James and I, after an appropriate courtship in front of my extremely romantic fireplace, moved upstairs to the Heliotrope Room, I realized that I didn't know his name, and I was horrified. When I was young and spent my life traveling up and down the eastern seaboard to dances and football games and long weekends, there was a terrible girl named Elise Finster. A terrible, trampy girl. Her roommate, Diana Hardaway, once told me that Elise had gone to bed with a man she didn't know. Didn't even know his name, just came dragging into her room at five in the morning with her formal barely hooked up, crying. "She doesn't even know his name," said Diana, and that shocked me. It seemed like that was the bottom line of decency, to know the name of the man you've slept with. Whenever I got worried about being decent, I said to myself, At least you're not like Elise Finster. At least you know their names. Not that there were so many, way back then. So, as I said, I was horrified when I realized that I didn't even know James's name. I mean, I knew he was either Sean Dapps or James Seltzer, because those were the names in the guest log, but I didn't know which was which. So I said, "Darling, I simply cannot take another step until you tell me your name. A lady has certain rules."

He gave me a strange glance, but he answered. "James," he said. "My name is James Seltzer." Then he kissed me, and, my, could that boy kiss, "Got any more rules?" he said, pressing me up against the door, "I love rules." What a fabulous boy!

After he and his friend Sean left the next morning, I got to thinking. I am sixty-two years old, although everyone says I don't look a day over fifty, and I don't expect that I will have another man in my life, particularly since Grangier Farm is in the middle of absolutely nowhere. I could be wrong, of course, since one never knows what the next hour will bring, but I seriously contemplated the possibility that James was going to be the last man for me. You see, I am not afraid to age. I thought about James; first about his marvelous hands and mouth; and then about his youth. Thirty, perhaps younger. Starting out in life. He had mentioned a business—what was it?—a design business, although I wasn't quite sure what that meant. By lunchtime, I had made my decision, and after carefully copying James's address from my guest book, I visited my lawyer, Wilman Stump. Wilman protested, of course, but he never could do a thing with me, which is why I retain him, and I changed my will to leave the proceeds of Grangier Farm to James Seltzer. Who else should I leave it to? Marcella? Ha! She has been an inconsiderate and greedy woman as long as I have known her, and it was only when Thomas's son died and she began to presume herself his heir that she showed up with her dreadful jam every week. Thomas couldn't abide her. So I left the property to James. He would be an ideal innkeeper should he decide to keep the place, but it's fine with me if he decides to sell it. Young men need money, and when I'm dead, I won't. I imagined his face when he received the news, and I almost relished the thought of death, so that I could give him that surprise. When I left Wilman's office, I felt better than I had in years.

●

I was pretty surprised when I got notice. I had almost forgotten that night. I called the lawyer right away. "She left it to me? Are you absolutely sure?"

He said he was. He said that she had changed the will several years before. I asked for the date, and he told me. It was the day after we stayed there. For a few hours I walked around my apartment, thinking about Lila. Had she taken a secret interest in me? Did she feel sorry for me because I had been left out? I couldn't figure it out. Then I thought about Sean, about the way he did things, and it came to me. He told her he was me. What an asshole! But what a break for me! I hadn't talked to Sean for a couple years, but I called him then.

"Hey Jim, man, what's up?" he said, like he hadn't noticed that we hadn't talked for two years.

"Hi Sean, I've just got a quick question for you, buddy. You remember that night at Grangier Farm? That bed and breakfast we went to after the Sterling presentation in Portland that time? Remember?"

"What farm?" asked Sean.

"Grangier Farm? Remember? Lila?"

"Lila, Lila. It's coming back to me. She was kind of old?"

"That's the one."

"Yeah, okay."

"Did you tell her you were me?" I said.

"What?"

"Did you tell her that your name was James Seltzer?" I asked, pretty impatient by now.

There was a little pause. "I think I did, man. Sorry. See, I just didn't want her calling—"

"Pretty nasty trick, buddy."

"Sorry, man. Sorry. What? Did she call you?"

"No, her lawyer called. She's dead."

"Oh. Oh well. She was pretty old."

"And she left me her property in her will." You prick, I almost said.

"Oh man, she did what?" Sean couldn't believe it.

"She left the whole place to me. The lawyer said it's worth over two million, if I want to sell it."

"Oh fuck." He was whispering now.

"Just thought I'd tell you she's dead," I said, and hung up. He called me back a few times, but I didn't answer.

Old dog, new Tricks

Mrs. Elsie Front had been known to say that she owed nothing to anyone. More than once, her bridge partners had heard about her bootstraps and how she had pulled herself up by them. "She's a real go-getter," said Mrs. Marjorie Euclaire enviously. Mrs. Marjorie Euclaire had been a secretary to a veterinarian in 1958, but since then she had been a homemaker, which always sounded strange to her, as though she had built the house herself. Elsie Front, on the other hand, had been, prior to her retirement, a career woman. Her career was in dolls, and she had been extremely successful. "I saw a need," she always said. This need was for dolls custom designed to look like the children who owned them. Doting relatives sent in a picture of the child and You're A Doll, Inc., took a standard doll's head and applied the requisite wig to it. They popped in appropriately colored eyeballs, and dotted the doll's skin with freckles or moles as desired. For an extra $175.00, they would supply matching outfits for child and doll. Children generally loathed their look-alike dolls (or suspected that their parents were going to kill them and keep the doll), but grandparents loved the whole concept, and Elsie Front raked it in.

In 1992, she sold You're A Doll, Inc., to GirlTime Toys for a whopping eleven million dollars and retired to the lap of luxury. The lap consisted of two new Jaguars and two annual shopping sprees in New York City, because if there was anything Elsie prided herself on, it was her style. "Just because we're senior citizens doesn't mean we have to let ourselves go," she said to Marjorie Euclaire, who looked guiltily down at her pink stretch pants (K-mart, $16.35). Elsie herself was in the midst of a leopard-spotted phase that had begun with a scarf and had burgeoned into dresses, two coats, blouses, silk pajamas, and, disastrously, capri pants. She even had a pair of leopard-spotted high heels with a matching handbag. Decked out in a form-fitting spotted dress and accessorized with spotted

heels and handbag as well as an elephantine diamond pin in the shape of a sprig of holly, Elsie Front was a sight to behold. She had had a face-lift in 1982, and her thin cheeks were taut and fiercely pink, but her forehead was creased with horizontal lines from frowning.

Frowning had been part of her job as the President and CEO of You're A Doll, Inc., but Elsie had done a fair amount of frowning since her retirement, too. The primary cause of her frowning was the news. In the morning she watched "Wake Up, America!" and "The Morning Show," and "It's a New Day," and at night she watched "The Ten O'Clock News" and "The Fitzjames Report." She read the *Wall Street Journal* religiously, as well as the local paper. As a result, she was incensed most of the time.

What Elsie Front was incensed by was the existence of what she called "the criminal element." She insisted that this had absolutely nothing to do with skin color—"No one can call me a bigot. I hired a number of black people in my day" (Actually, the number was seven, and they were all janitorial staff)—but, she said, certain statistics could not be ignored. The poverty excuse was, she said, a sham and a ruse. "Whine, whine, whine. Complain, complain, complain," she said angrily to Marjorie. "They should stop fussing and get a job. Look! Look!" she rattled the want ads, "the paper is filled with jobs. Employers are begging for workers! And these people just sit around asking for welfare. Why, when I had my company, I was desperate for people who could work, desperate! Nobody wanted to work. They'd come in and start talking about their coffee break, their lunch break—that's all they cared about, I'll tell you! Lazy! That's what they are!"

Marjorie nodded, but sometimes she thought Elsie went too far. She felt this especially when Elsie berated homeless people in the street. It just didn't seem right. Elsie would pass a ragged man holding a sign saying something along the lines of "Will work for food. Please help," and she'd stop and lecture him. "Get up and work then! The papers are filled with jobs! Go get a paper and make something out of yourself, for heaven's sake! I started a company and built it up myself, without begging and with good hard work, and now I'm a millionaire. I pulled myself up by my bootstraps, and you expect me to believe that you can't find a job! Nonsense!" And she would stride off in her high heels. Marjorie usually gave the man a few dollars while apologizing for her friend's behavior.

Given her feelings about the criminal element, it was no surprise that Elsie Front did not like New York City. "If it wasn't for Saks, I'd never go, " she said. The city was a dangerous place where terrible things happened to the unsuspecting. Luckily, Elsie was not the unsuspecting. Only a few years ago, she had read in the paper about a criminal who crept into the hotel rooms of lone, elderly women. There he lurked beneath their beds until they were sound asleep and then—"well, you can imagine." The problem, Elsie always said, was that the neighborhoods had become too mixed. "Before," she said, "people stayed in their own neighborhoods, with their own people. Everything was fine. Now, you don't know who you're going to run into, even downtown. Sometimes even in the same restaurant." Accordingly, Elsie did not patronize the restaurants of New York City. She shopped from 11 a.m. until 5:30 p.m., and then she restored herself to her suite at the Regent Hotel, where she ordered room service and watched the news. Usually she made a call of complaint to the front desk (one time, room service had taken an hour) and turned in by 10:30.

On day three of Elsie's final trip to New York City, she entered the Regent elevator from the fifteenth floor promptly at 10:53 a.m., attired in a symphony of spots and ready for a day of consumption. Absorbed in various sartorial adjustments, Elsie was not conscious of the elevator's descent until it slowed to a stop on the tenth floor, and the unthinkable occurred. A tall black man wearing a large overcoat stepped into the elevator. Elsie Front let out a sharp gasp, but the man remained impassive. Her worst fears were confirmed when she saw that he was accompanied by an evil-looking Doberman pinscher. The criminal element! Silently, he edged toward the back of the car.

I haven't got much time, thought Elsie, just as the man lifted his arm threateningly.

"Down, lady," he commanded.

Elsie Front collapsed upon the floor and waited for the worst to happen. The seconds passed with excruciating slowness; she pictured him gloating over her prone body. Then the elevator door opened. The man stepped carefully around Elsie and disembarked.

"Come, lady," he said. The dog trotted after him. He did not look back.

Elsie reached a single finger upward and pressed a button. She did not arise until she had reached the fifteenth floor, where she walked slowly to her room. For nearly an hour she sat on the edge of her bed feeling, for the first time in her life, shame.

Babysitters' Club

It wasn't that the house was so huge. It was big, but the problem was the way it was big. Perched against the side of a hill, and old, so that the shingles shivered when the wind blew, and with half a dozen balconies cropping out of the house when you least expected them, it was big in a nerve-wracking way. At the top was the attic bedroom, where Mr. and Mrs. Deetz slept. A thin black staircase led up to that room from the kitchen, and you could hear someone whistling up there when you knew that nobody was in the room. That was weird, and so was the closet at the top of the stairs, where for some reason Mrs. Deetz kept her wedding gown; when you opened the closet, the heavy white satin seemed to push out toward you and wrap around your ankles. If you panicked, it felt as though the dress was pulling you into the closet.

But it was easy to avoid the top of the house, and sometimes you could stop thinking about the top floor for a couple hours at a time. It was the middle floor that was the real problem. There was no getting away from it, that's for sure, because that's where the kids, Janie and Martin, slept. You couldn't just sit in front of the TV and tell them to go on up to bed by themselves, because they were scared, too. The number-one thing that was wrong with the middle floor was that there were two staircases to get to it, the front one and the back one. Now, of course, nobody in their right mind would take the back stairs, because Mrs. Deetz, God knows why, had hung a thick curtain against the wall that the stairs ran next to. It was blue plush and maybe she thought it was elegant. She had probably seen it on the Home and Garden channel. But it was like walking inside a cotton ball—no sound came in or out. You knew that no one could hear you scream when you climbed those stairs. It was dark, too. So, obviously, you took the front stairs, going up with the kids to their bedrooms. The front stairs were okay, bright and everything, but always at the back of your mind, you remembered that there were two staircases. You couldn't be both places at once, could you? And that was only the beginning.

The next bad thing was the water in the bathroom. It would go on for no reason— swoosh! In the middle of the night, the water would come rushing out of the faucet in the tub, and you'd have to go up and turn it off. It would also change temperature with no warning. The

kids would be brushing their teeth, and you'd be checking the mirror to make sure of what was behind you, and all of a sudden one of them would cry out because the water had turned scalding hot. When it turned cold, it wasn't so bad.

The kids always wanted to sleep in the same room. They begged to sleep in the same room. Marty went down on his knees once. Mrs. Deetz didn't allow that, though. She said it made her nuts to think of how much they'd paid for a house with enough bedrooms and then have everyone sleeping together. Still, you hated to see their faces when you said no. We all let them keep their lights on, as bright as they wanted.

Downstairs wasn't so great, either, but that's where the door was. You knew that you could get out if you had to. When I was there, I always looked out the front door a few times, just to reassure myself. The downstairs seemed pretty regular, really, except for the kitchen, which smelled like bacon. That doesn't sound so bad, right? Bacon's not such a bad smell, right? It was foul. The air in the kitchen was thick with burning bacon and you could feel the droplets of grease on your face. Sometimes when you opened the door, a gust of smoke would come out, practically choking you, and after you came out, your clothes would smell of bacon. I asked Janie one time if they ate a lot of bacon, and she rolled her eyes at me. "We're Jewish. We don't eat bacon." Okay, and add to that the basement room. The basement was down below, and next to it was a bedroom with nothing in it except a bed. I think it was supposed to be a guest room, even though you'd have to be crazy to sleep there. There was a long, dark set of stairs leading up from the basement into the kitchen. Of course, you locked the door the minute the Deetzes left, but still, you knew it was there.

Obviously, the question that comes to mind is why did we go there? The main reason was that the Deetzes paid double, $14.00 an hour. We were thirteen and fourteen—we weren't going to get that kind of money anywhere else. Also, they were smart enough to diversify. Mrs. Deetz taught at our school, Collington Academy, so she had a big pool to choose from. She'd only call you about once every four months, and by that time you had sort of forgotten how scared you'd been and just remembered the $10.00 an hour. The Deetzes had a great TV and lots of videos, too. And I have to say, the fact that there was always chocolate cake in the fridge was kind of a draw. Most people had Nutter Butters at best. Janie and Marty were okay kids, too. They didn't expect you to play with them or kiss them goodnight or anything. We just watched TV and ate cake together. They were less annoying than a lot of kids.

But we never thought that Missy Trainor would go to the Deetz's. She was the scared-est person we knew. We always said that she brought most of it on herself, watching movies like *Rosemary's Baby* and reading those magazines about quadriplegic arsonists and wolf-children. Once in English class, we saw *To Kill a Mockingbird*, and Missy screamed when Boo Radley came out from behind the door. She was a bundle of nerves. She once told us that she was afraid of nail-polish remover, so we couldn't believe it when she said, at lunch, that she was going to sit for the Deetz kids on Saturday night. We practically choked. Mary Harness, who was kind of nasty, said, "You know it's haunted, don't you?"

"Oh, that's just a big rumor," said Missy, but she was already getting pale.

"Just wait till you hear the whistling," said Mary Harness, all snide.

"You don't always hear it," said Mary Canning, trying to be comforting.

"Why on earth are you babysitting up at the Deetz's?" I asked.

"I want the money," whispered Missy. "I want to take scuba lessons."

Well, the thought of Missy's puny white face peering out of a scuba mask was so funny that we all busted up, and Missy got mad and left in a huff, not that I blame her.

She didn't talk to us for the rest of the week, but we heard she was asking some of the other girls if they'd come with her to the Deetz's. Of course, she didn't get any takers—$7.00 an hour is not enough to be that scared—but her cousin Bernadette finally agreed to come along. Bernadette weighed about 200 pounds and was chronically exasperated. She thought everything was stupid, especially Missy. Bernadette sat next to me the day they showed *To Kill a Mockingbird*, and when Missy screamed, Bernadette said, under her breath, "I'm going to stick a pair of scissors in *your* leg if you don't shut up." That was pretty funny, but sometimes Bernadette could be mean; in first grade, she told everyone when she found out that Santa Claus wasn't real. Some kids cried.

We heard the story a couple of months later from Missy herself. She didn't want to talk about it at first, but we told her we had a right to know, since we had been babysitters for the Deetzes too, so she told us the whole story. She said that when she got there, she was already shaking because of all the things she'd heard. Bernadette whopped her on the back and said, "Don't be a such a weenie! Stop it!" She did all the talking to Mrs. Deetz about bedtime and phone numbers and stuff. Missy said she didn't hear a thing, she was so busy looking around for evidence of poltergeists. She didn't see anything, but she was still scared. After Mr. and Mrs. Deetz left, Bernadette stomped all over the house, dragging Missy behind her. "Look," she said. "Here's the living room. See? No ghosts. And here's the TV room. No blood on the floor." Janie and Martin followed them, just looking. They didn't say anything. When they finally got to the kitchen, Missy said, "Everyone says we should lock the door to the downstairs. That's what they all do."

"Everyone's an idiot," said Bernadette. "Right, kids?" She smiled at Janie and Martin.

"I'd lock it," said Janie.

"Sheesh. You guys all watch too many movies. Let's have some of this chocolate cake I've been hearing about," said Bernadette. So they each cut themselves a big wedge of cake and went to the TV room. Missy said she stopped being so scared then. It just seemed regular, and she began to wonder what we had been talking about. She thought maybe we had been pulling her leg. The kitchen didn't smell like bacon and she couldn't hear any whistling.

"So we had some cake with the kids and watched TV. They seemed like nice kids. Austin Powers was on HBO, and that was pretty funny, so it seemed like nothing—like a regular house."

But then they heard the stairs. It was just the tiniest creaking on the stairs that led from the basement to the kitchen. Like somebody was trying not to be heard.

Then Janie looked over at Martin and said, "Here we go."

He just kept his eyes on the television, but you could tell he wasn't really watching. "Lock the door in the kitchen," he said to Missy in a soft voice.

Missy couldn't move. She said her heart was about to pop through her chest and her legs were frozen. She shook her head.

"You," he said to Bernadette.

"You what?" said Bernadette. "I'm not going to lock that door. It's an old house and it's doing what old houses do, which is creaking. Jeez. You guys are wimps." She munched her cake.

Missy started to think that she was smelling bacon. She didn't want Bernadette to bawl her out, so she tried to sniff unobtrusively.

"Whatsamatter?" asked Bernadette. "You got a cold?"

Janie scooted close to Martin and whispered in his ear. "Martin and I have to go to bed now," she said. "You two come with us," she said to Missy and Bernadette.

"Um. Okay. It's only eight, though. You sure?"

"Yes. You come with us. We'll go by the front stairs."

Missy said that the bathroom, where they brushed their teeth, was normal. Scalding water didn't come spurting out.

"Janie and I are sleeping in my room," said Martin firmly. Missy protested, like Mrs. Deetz had told her to, but they just looked at her impassively. After she stopped talking, they turned together and disappeared into Martin's bedroom. Missy could hear the lock snap into place.

"Goodnight," she called through the door.

"Goodnight," they answered politely.

When she was at the top of the stairs, Janie opened the door. "Don't go upstairs," she said to Missy. "To my parent's room. Don't go up there." She closed the door and the lock snapped again.

"Scaredy-cat kids," said Bernadette as they returned to the TV room. "If I was their mother, I'd put a stop to that. Phew. Stinks in here."

It smelled like bacon, Missy said, but not exactly like bacon, either. More like burning grease.

She started shaking again, but Bernadette was just irritated. "Don't even tell me," she sighed, "You're too scared to go to the kitchen to check the stove. God almighty." And off she went. Missy could hear her feet thumping through the house for a minute and then there was a silence that lasted a long time.

She came back shaking her head. "It's a wonder the house didn't burn down. There was a frying pan just burning on the stove. Big clouds of smoke coming out. I bet the whole kitchen would've caught fire in a few minutes."

"But there wasn't any burner on when we were in there, Bern. There wasn't."

"Oh, there probably was. Or maybe one of those weirdo kids came down and did it to scare you. We'll just tell Mrs. Deetz she should be more careful with the stove." Bernadette was nonchalant.

"I'm really scared, Bern. This house is haunted."

"Missy, you're always really scared. Remember the time you thought the Easter egg was going to explode?"

"It looked funny," Missy said defensively.

"You're the one who looked funny, running away from an egg," Bernadette said, laughing.

"But there's something weird about this house. I can feel it."

" 'I can feeeeeel it.' You're a goon."

The telephone began to ring. Missy leapt up out of her chair and looked wildly around. Bernadette rolled her eyes and walked over to a small desk that held a phone.

"Hello, Deetz residence," she said in her gravelly voice. But there was no one on the line. She stared at the receiver. Somewhere in the house, a phone was still ringing. "Oh well," she shrugged. "The machine will pick up."

But the Deetzes didn't seem to have a machine. The ringing went on and on, distant yet insistent.

"These have got to be the most annoying people in the world," Bernadette growled. "Who doesn't have a machine anymore?'

Missy couldn't answer. Her throat was closed in terror.

The phone rang and rang.

Even Bernadette began to look nonplussed. "What's the deal here?" she murmured. "Maybe it's the Deetzes calling."

The phone rang on.

"Oh for God's sake, I'm going to go find that goddamn phone."

"Don't go," Missy managed to say.

"What?"

"Don't go anywhere."

"Jesus H. Christ. Don't you want that phone to stop?"

"Just don't go anywhere," said Missy with her teeth clenched to stop their chattering.

"Oh, spare me. You get to stay here. I'm the one who has to traipse all over the house. I bet the stupid phone is in their bedroom. Sheesh."

"The kids said not to go up there." Missy said, starting to panic.

"Blah blah. They're weirdoes. I'm going to find the phone. It's driving me crazy."

"I'm going to call the police if you go up there," said Missy, struggling for power.

"Oh yeah," said Bernadette disdainfully. "Right. What phone are you going to use?"

She strode out of the room, and, Missy said, it was as though she had disappeared.

There were no footsteps. It was like she had been sucked away. Missy had been telling the truth when she said she would call the police. She had every intention of doing it, but she said that a strange thing happened when Bernadette left. She went into a trance.

"It was like fainting except that every few minutes I would wake up and think 'I've got to get up and call the police, but I couldn't get my legs to work. I can't figure out how long that went on. Five minutes or half an hour? I don't know. I couldn't move. I couldn't hear anything. It was like I was drowning in cushions, going under for the last time. And then I heard her scream. It was just one scream, but it went on and on and on. God, it was awful. Without thinking I was on my feet and running through the house. I didn't even realize it, but I was running up to the second floor. When I got there, the hall was pitch black, and I was brushing my fingers along the wall, trying to find a light. Finally, I found the switch, but when I flipped it—nothing. Then I could feel my heart start beating like crazy, wham wham wham. I was wet with sweat—I wanted to run for the front door, but I kept thinking 'Got to find a phone, got to call the police.' But it was so dark.

"Then I saw a light. It was dim because it was coming from the upstairs bedroom. I could hardly see anything, but I stood at the bottom of that little black staircase, listening. Something was slamming against the walls. I stood there, but I was stuck. I couldn't go up and I couldn't run away. I couldn't move. Then the door to the bedroom opened. I couldn't really see, because it was pretty dark, but I could hear it open. All the slamming stopped, and I turned around and ran.

"I heard this little giggle, and then there was a sound like a ball bouncing after me, but I was running down the hall, past Janie and Martin's rooms, toward the front stairs. I stumbled down those, with the ball chasing after me, bump bump bump. I was heading right for the door, I didn't care about anyone else anymore, but when I reached the doorknob, I turned around to look—I guess I felt like I was almost safe so it was okay—and saw what was rolling down the stairs after me. It was Bernadette's head. Just her head, toppling over and over, turning around the landing on the staircase like it knew where it was going. Bumping down the stairs toward where I stood. I saw that her mouth was open, like she was still screaming. It bumped into my feet before I could pull the door open."

He had been living in the basement room for months, the guy who killed Bernadette. Of course, the first thing we thought was, it could have been me. But it turned out that maybe it couldn't have been anyone but Bernadette. He had been listening to them, and when the police asked him why he killed her, he just laughed. He said, "She didn't believe in ghosts." He was skinny and pale, because he had been living in the dark for so long, and we wondered how he could have done it. I mean, she was a big person. The police said that she had died of a heart attack. That he had actually scared her to death.

We were surprised that the Deetzes didn't move after that. They stayed there for about three more years, until Mr. Deetz was transferred to Chicago. Of course, no one would babysit for them after that. I guess they just stayed home.

Twice daily, after meals

Once upon a time, the Cones went to France. Before France, they went to England, Ireland, Denmark, Holland, Germany, Switzerland, Austria, Italy, and Spain. That took seventeen days. Paris was their final stop—they were giving it a leisurely three days. They were just checking into their hotel.

"HI! I'M AL CONE AND I HAVE A RESERVATION. DO YOU SPEAK ENGLISH?"

"Yes, monsieur. And your name is Mr. Cone?" said the desk clerk, tapping at his computer.

"C-O-N-E. CONE! CONE!"

"It's cute," said Marcella Cone, looking around the lobby.

"It better be cute, for how much it cost, I'll tell you that," said Al Cone.

"Monsieur Cone, I have for your family a reservation for three rooms, all with double bed—"

"OH NO YOU DON'T, NO SIR! I ORDERED A KING-SIZE BED."

"Monsieur Cone, we have no king-size bed. We have two double beds in a room, but we have no king-size bed."

"SO NOW YOU TELL ME. YOU WAIT UNTIL I'M HERE AND I CAN'T GO ANY-WHERE ELSE AND THEN YOU TELL ME. DON'T THINK I'M NOT ONTO YOU."

"Monsieur Cone, please to refer to our letter of April twenty-third, in which we confirm your reservation for three rooms with double beds." The clerk waved a piece of paper in the general direction of Al Cone. "You see?"

"Mine better have a TV," said Fitz Cone.

"DOES HIS HAVE A TV?" bellowed Al Cone, switching campaigns.

"Monsieur Cone, all of our rooms contain television," said the clerk soothingly.

Marcella Cone nudged her husband with her elbow. "View," she muttered.

"AND WE'D BETTER NOT HAVE A VIEW OF AN AIRSHAFT. WE HAD A VIEW OF AN AIRSHAFT IN ROME AND WE'D BETTER NOT HAVE ONE HERE WITH THE KIND OF PRICES YOU'RE CHARGING. AND IT BETTER BE CLEAN, TOO."

The clerk sighed. "One room views on the street and the others are outlooking to our garden. Our rooms are cleaned each day."

"WHY CAN'T WE HAVE THEM ALL TOGETHER WITH A VIEW OF THE GARDEN. THAT'S WHAT I WANT! THREE GARDEN-VIEW ROOMS!"

"Very well, Monsieur Cone, I will give you three garden-view rooms. In one room, Monsieur and Madame Cone, in another the two young ladies, and the third for this young gentleman. Correct?"

"WELL, HE'S NOT MUCH OF A GENTLEMAN, ARE YOU, FITZ?"

"Shut up, Dad."

"BUT OTHERWISE THAT SOUNDS RIGHT. LET'S TALK MONEY NOW. WE'RE STAYING THREE NIGHTS AND I THINK THAT ENTITLES ME TO A BREAK. WHAT CAN YOU DO FOR ME?"

"A break?"

"DON'T PRETEND YOU DON'T UNDERSTAND ME. A BREAK! A DISCOUNT! BECAUSE WE'RE STAYING SO LONG. A SAVINGS!"

"Monsieur Cone, we do not have this kind of thing, this break," said the clerk grimly.

"FIVE HUNDRED FRANCS A NIGHT! THAT'S OUTRAGEOUS! I BET THE BATH-ROOMS ARE FILTHY, TOO. YOU'D NEVER GET AWAY WITH THIS IN THE STATES!" He turned to his wife, "Marcella, let's go somewhere else. This place is a pigsty. Kids, come on."

"Oh honey, let's stay. It's cute. It's so cute. Look at those windows. They're French windows. Get it?" Marcella pleaded.

"Da-ad. Remember Amsterdam? Remember how we couldn't find another hotel?" whined Shelley.

"Remember how you promised you wouldn't do that again?" whined Julieanne.

"Yeah, Dad. Chill," said Fitz.

"You kids think that money grows on trees. Fifteen hundred francs a night! That's over three hundred dollars! For nothing, too. They probably clean the toilets once a year. I'LL TELL YOU," he said, turning towards the desk clerk, "IN THE STATES YOU CAN GET A PERFECTLY GOOD ROOM FOR $34.95 A NIGHT. WITH CLEAN SHEETS! EUROPE IS A RIP-OFF AND I'M GOING TO ADVISE MY FRIENDS AT HOME NOT TO COME. THE PLACE IS A GYP. DON'T PRETEND YOU DON'T UNDERSTAND ME.

"On the contrary, Monsieur Cone, I understand perfectly. Do you wish to stay?"

"Come on, Al, please. It's so cute."

"GODDAMMIT. ALL RIGHT. THERE BETTER NOT BE FUNGUS IN THE POT OR I'M

OUT OF HERE. LET ME TELL YOU," he turned to his children, "This is the only goddamn European vacation you're getting."

"Bummer," said Fitz tonelessly.

"SHUT YOUR MOUTH, YOUNG MAN," thundered Al. "LET'S GET THESE GOD-DAMN BAGS TO THE ROOM, HUH? WHERE'S THE BELLBOY!"

The clerk rang a tiny bell. "Alain! Venez ici!"

•

I dislike all Americans, but these are the kind of Americans I dislike the most. Fat and red and full of complaints. Complaining about how tiny the elevator is. Complaining about how it is so slow. And how hungry they are. And they want it now now now. The very minute they desire a thing, it should appear. Like children. I should be complaining, not them, because they have the heaviest baggage in the universe. Americans cannot pack a little sack and go—again, they must have everything they want, instantly—so they bring twenty pairs of shoes. It is a mystery why the people who have so many bags full of clothes look so terrible, but they do. These Cones looked especially terrible, the madame with her brown pantsuit, the girls so ugly in bellbottoms that drag to the floor and too-tight t-shirts, the little boy in the Beavis and Butthead shirt. Worst of all was the father, with his big stomach falling out of his shirt and his hairy knees coming out of his shorts. I hated him the most, for while the others complained about the elevator and their hunger, the father stared at me with his beady eyes. I look to the ceiling, I look to the floor, I look to the baggage, but he all the time has his eyes on me. Finally he says, practically shouting, "I'm watching you like a hawk, buddy, so don't try anything funny."

I say, "Pardon me?"

He says, "I've heard the stories about you guys. I know your tricks. You might be thinking about opening one of these bags and just helping yourself, but I'm on to you. I know all about it."

I don't say anything, but I am even madder than ever. He is saying that I am a thief! How I hate this man! If I was a thief, I would be rich enough to quit this stupid job here. I want to hit him, but I think of my job. I have to think very hard.

Now he is saying more. "Just stay away from the camera, bub. That's a Minolta, and I bet you could get a pretty penny for it over here, but you can just forget it."

He accuses me of stealing his camera, his Minolta. I would not want such a camera, and now I am even more insulted. I am thinking that I might hit him anyway, when one of the ugly girls says, "Daddy, don't be crabby. He's just doing his job."

"Hah!" says the father. "I'm on to this guy."

So we arrive at the fifth floor, and they get out of the elevator like a pack of elephants, not a single one offering to help with the baggage. "Where's our room? Which ones are ours!" they're yelling the whole time, while I'm trying to push their bags. Then they have to decide which one gets this room, which one gets that room. They don't like this bed, they don't like those curtains. Monsieur Cone is sniffing the bathrooms, looking in the toilets. They turn on all the televisions instantly. How I hate this family. Then they fight each other about the bags—this one is mine, don't touch it. Leave me alone! Stop fighting, kids! Finally, I get all their baggage to the correct room. Naturally, I go to Monsieur Cone's room last. I deliver his six bags, including his ridiculous camera, and then I wait.

"There's mildew in the shower! I can smell it!"

"Oh, Al," says madame, "It's perfectly charming."

"That's what you always say, Marcella. The place is a sty."

When he stops sniffing, I say, "Is there anything more, Monsieur Cone?" He must certainly know what he is supposed to do.

"No," he says.

I wait again.

After a minute, he turns to me and says, "You're waiting for a tip, aren't you? I guess I'm supposed to tip you because you didn't steal from me, right? Goddamn Europe. Okay, bud, here's your tip," and he gives me a dollar bill. One dollar bill. I look at him, and he shrugs, "It's better than your money, that's for sure. At least you know it'll be worth something tomorrow."

That is when I have my marvelous idea. I think to myself that my job is so not important as this marvelous idea.

"What're you smiling about, bud? Don't you have something else to do?" says this Cone.

"Yes, monsieur," say I, but I cannot stop smiling.

●

Marcella Cone swept into Le Petit Grotto at 12:05. "Sue! Mimi! Excusez-moi for being so en retard. I just had to take two seconds to pick up our photos from Paris, because I knew you'd want to see them. I haven't even taken a peek yet myself, and I'm just dying."

Sue and Mimi eyed her bleakly. "Oh yes. How was your trip?"

"Fabulous! Whirlwind! But fabulous! We did England, Ireland, Denmark, Holland, Germany, Switzerland, Austria, Italy, Spain, and, of course, Paris. All in three weeks! We landed in London at around ten-thirty in the morning on Sunday the twenty-first. Well, I have to tell you, we were all so jet-lagged that Al said, 'Let's just take a taxi into town,' because, of course, we were at Heathrow, which is about forty miles from the actual city. It took ages to get our bags, but customs was a breeze. Al says it pays to be American, even though he was the one who was so worried about things being confiscated. Well, whatever. Anyway, the taxi ride was just something, what with being on the other side of the road. I just had to laugh because Al kept yelling 'Watch out!' I'll tell you, it was something dangerous just to try to cross the street, you know, because you have to look in the other direction to see the cars coming. Fitz just couldn't keep it in his mind, and my heart was in my throat four or five different times. But that was later. Let me tell you about the hotel. The brochure had said 'Charming bed and breakfast with cozy rooms.' Well, they were cozy all right—about ten feet square is all they were. And the bathroom all the way down the hall. And it didn't smell too nice, either, if you know what I mean. Al just about blew a gasket when he saw it. 'You call this charming?!' The girl didn't know what to say. So of course, we didn't stay there. We went up the street—"

"Don't you want to order something?" Mimi broke in hopefully. The waitress was staring at Marcella.

"Oh, just a salad. Just any old salad. A Caesar salad. But no anchovies."

"We can remove them, Ma'am."

"Yes, do that. What kind of dressing?"

"Um, Caesar."

"Oh, right. Yes, I'll have that—without the anchovies, remember," said Marcella, shaking her finger playfully at the waitress. "I can't stand anchovies. They're so fishy. Anyway, we found this cute little hotel just up the block. It was called the Staunton Arms, I think. Or maybe the Stanford Arms. I can't remember. Our room had the prettiest wallpaper, too, little tiny pink roses on this trellis stripe, I think it was a sort of forest green. Anyway—"

"Let's look at your pictures before lunch comes, Marcella. It would be terrible if we got food on them," said Sue loudly.

"Oh, that's good thinking, Sue," said Marcella, "even though Paris was at the end of our trip and I'm only at the beginning. I sort of hate to go out of order, but I'd die if I got salad dressing on these. These are our memories." She pulled a packet from her gigantic straw purse.

"So you just have pictures of Paris? What about the rest of the trip?"

Marcella looked annoyed. "Well, this was the last roll, so it was just ready today, and Al took all the rest of the photos to his office today, even though I told him you two would be just sick about not getting to see them. He said you could see them next week. We took hundreds, and even though some of them are a little out of focus and whatnot, you can still see all the sights and things."

"Hum," said Mimi weakly, "But this is just Paris, right?"

"Just Paris, which is a shame. But I guess we're lucky to have them at all, because the camera was nearly stolen in Paris. At least, we think so. It was the strangest thing. Right after we arrived at this little hotel, the Hotel Sancerre, we were so hungry we were about to die. Luckily, there was a Hard Rock Café right around the corner, so we went and had some burgers. Well, when we came back," Marcella's voice dropped to a conspiratorial whisper, "the camera was lying on the bed with the tripod next to it. Now, you know Al;

he keeps his camera safe in the case all the time. He's real fussy about it, won't let any of the kids touch it, cleans it with those little cloths—he's just real fussy about it. So there it was on the bed, and Al says, 'Did one of you kids mess with my Minolta?' They all say no, and you know, our kids don't lie, so we didn't know what to make of it. Al was furious, even though there didn't seem to be anything wrong with the camera and the film was still in and all. He called the embassy to complain. It was hours before he calmed down, but later, he figured out that a thief had come in the window and tried to steal the camera, but had been scared away, you know, by us coming back."

"Well, that's lucky," said Sue. "That the camera didn't get stolen."

"I guess so," said Marcella, "But it was a close call. And they're always talking about crime in America! Al gave them a piece of his mind at the hotel. He said he was going to take them to court, but I guess, really, since nothing was actually stolen, that wouldn't make sense. Having that near-brush, though, we took plenty of pictures in Paris. You know how we feel about photos—these are our memories." She opened the envelope and set the stack on the table. "Now Sue, just move your chair over here, so we can all see together. Can you see, Mimi?"

"Uh-huh," said Mimi sullenly.

The first picture was a thumb. "That's a thumb," said Sue.

"Sometimes Al forgets his thumb," said Marcella.

The second picture seemed to be of a ceiling. "What's this?" said Marcella, blankly.

"It looks like a ceiling," said Mimi.

"I can see that," snapped Marcella. "It's the ceiling of our hotel room. Al wouldn't take a picture of the ceiling of our hotel room." She flipped to the next photo and stopped. "Oh!" she cried. It was a blurry image, but it was unmistakably a bottom, the naked bottom of a thin man. "Oh no!" Marcella gasped.

Mimi reached out and flipped to the next picture. This picture was in perfect focus. It was the same naked bottom, but this time, the handle of a red toothbrush protruded from it.

"That's my toothbrush!" shrieked Marcella.

Sue flipped to the next picture. This time, the a green toothbrush emerged from the hairy asshole.

"That's Al's!" Marcella moaned.

In the next photo, three toothbrushes were lodged jauntily where their predecessors had been.

"The kids!" sobbed Marcella.

"My goodness!" said Sue. "How do you imagine—?" She left the sentence unfinished.

"Oh, I hate Paris! I hate Paris!" Marcella wept.

Easy
Rider

Rahmid Al-Fahid, the sheep-herding king of Southern Tunisia, got fed up and moved to Los Angeles. After all, why not? He had more money than anyone in Southern Tunisia—he had enough money to buy the whole region if he wanted to, which he didn't. He couldn't think of a place he wanted to buy less than Southern Tunisia. Tunisia drove him crazy. There was the clerical problem, of course—can't do this, can't do that, at least not in public—but the pressing issues were practical. Plumbing, for instance. Here he was with six bathrooms. Six. Four of them had exquisite Venetian gold-plated faucets and drains, not that the other two were cheap looking, by any means, and what happened? He couldn't get the water hookup. He had virtually no water in five of the six bathrooms, and the sixth didn't work if someone was washing dishes in the kitchen. He even had to send one of the maids to the well on occasion. And that was just one thing. Electricity was variable, garbage service was variable, and chlorine for his pool was nonexistent, because, even though Rahmid ordered it special from Ron's Pool Party in Piastre, New Jersey, the sole shipping service that delivered to Southern Tunisia was Darcy's Worldwide, which was notable only for the drug consumption of its drivers. Not to mention that Rahmid's chauffeur was just sitting around playing poker with the cook because there was a spark plug shortage in Tunisia and the next shipment of spark plugs was coming overland from Liberia. Like I said, Tunisia drove him crazy.

So he moved to L.A. Specifically, he moved into a mansion on Sunset Boulevard. It had all the conveniences, and what's more, they worked. The water, the lights, the pool service—they all turned on and off and showed up at the right time. The garbage disposal ground things up. The mail appeared in its box each day. The telephone called the exact person he dialed. The maid went to the store and came back with the very things he wanted. Mostly, he liked frozen food. Frozen food knocked him out. There it was, frozen, in your freezer until you needed it. Then you took it out, put it in the microwave, and ate it, with nothing ever to remind you that it was frozen moments before. So efficient. The gardener came when he said he was going to come. The large pothole at the bottom of Rahmid's driveway was filled without Rahmid having to pay a cent for it.

For a long time after he moved to Los Angeles, Rahmid was happy. As time passed, though, he began to feel that he was, well, un-American. He saw in the movies that Americans were kings of the open road, conquerors of the great unknown, daredevils, drifters, and dreamers. They were pioneers, they were home on the range. They needed land, lots of land, and the starry sky above, don't fence me in. This was very interesting to Rahmid. In Tunisia, a starry sky above was déclassé, and for sure, you wanted to be fenced in (or rather, to have everyone else fenced out). But, Rahmid reflected, Americans needed to roam. Apparently, they needed to get into their cars and hit the road; there was very definitely something important about cars to Americans.

This, to Rahmid, was a delicate point. He didn't know how to drive. In Tunisia, of course, everyone of any standing or cash at all had a chauffeur, and now, in Los Angeles, he had two: Howard and Epps. He got everywhere he wanted to go, but this was insufficient. He should be speeding though the wide open spaces in a convertible with his amrah flapping behind him.

Accordingly, he began driving lessons with Epps. Sometimes he tried driving with Howard, but Howard was given to sharp screams every time Rahmid made a tiny little mistake, which was kind of nerve-wracking, so mostly he learned from Epps. He got his license in no time. He still couldn't exactly parallel park, and he tended to think that he had the right-of-way at every inter-section, but he had a license and the road was his oyster.

A road trip was naturally the next step. The Grand Canyon. Wyoming. All those places that Americans were always going. Just Rahmid and the open highway. And, certainly, the car. What kind of car, though, was the question. A convertible, which had seemed so appropriate in the begin-ning, now sounded rather confining. So small. Where would one put one's luggage? And now that he was so attached to frozen food, it seemed a shame to go for weeks without it. The starry sky above sounded nice in the song, but Rahmid pictured bugs on his face, which would be very unpleasant. Then he discovered recreational vehicles. A fabulous solution! A car that was also a house! Rahmid was overjoyed. He and Epps drove down to Beverly Hills RV, and Rahmid nearly bought two, they were so cute. The little sink. The little freezer. The little toilet. The comfortable bed with the win-dow for viewing the starry sky above. The little shelves and cabinets. After much scrutinizing, Rahmid settled on the Open Road Spectacular, which had the biggest gas tank and the most capacious freezer. He bought it right off the lot and drove it home that very day. Epps got a little rattled as he drove the Open Road Spectacular up Rodeo Drive toward Sunset ("Stay in your lane," Epps repeat-ed tediously), but Rahmid had never been happier or more pleased with his new country.

"Leave it to America," he told his brother over the phone that night.

"What?" said his brother. It was a typical Tunisian connection.

"Americans build the best machines in the world. Like the microwave, for instance. Like the Post-It note. A brilliant solution!"

"WHAT?"

"And now I have a car that's a house. I can drive over the beautiful American freeways and never be without comfort. If I get hungry, I can get up and make a sandwich. Thirsty, I reach into my refrigerator for a drink. Tired, I simply go to my bed. This is a country that makes life worth living!"

"YOU ARE HUNGRY?"

"No, no. I'll send you a postcard from Wyoming, Hassan. This connection is no good." He hung up and ruminated on the virtues of a well-ordered society.

Two days later, he set out for his adventure. The maid had purchased as much frozen food as she could squeeze into his freezer, plus potato chips, which Rahmid understood were essential, and a cooler of Pepsi. He was further outfitted with a gun, some hiking boots, and an umbrella, as well as a map of the entire country. He thought a lot about it and decided he would start by driving up the coast. The great Pacific Ocean was undoubtedly a sight not to be missed, and, besides, if he got bored, he could turn east and head toward Wyoming. Satisfied, he started the engine.

Driving without Epps was considerably more stressful than driving with Epps. Epps had let him know about red lights that were coming up, and without him, Rahmid missed a few. This was most dangerous, he knew, but he was taken aback by the fury of his fellow drivers. You would think they would try to be encouraging, but instead, they shouted at him and made violent noises with their cars.

Finally, though, he made his way through Santa Monica and on to the Pacific Coast Highway. It was everything he had dreamed of: the ocean sparkled off into the horizon on one side and the cliffs veered dizzily up on the other. This was undoubtedly the open road, and Rahmid was deeply gratified. That lasted until Ventura. The ocean sparkled, the cliffs veered, but that's all they did, and Rahmid began to get a little bored. That's when he started fiddling around with the dashboard buttons of the Open Road Spectacular. Emergency lights were interesting, and he squirted his windshield wiper fluid vigorously. Then he saw a button called "Cruise." As far as he knew, Cruise was something having to do with boats and water. Perhaps the Open Road Spectacular could float. Fascinated, he pulled to the side of the road and groped for his owner's manual. "Cruise control enables the driver to maintain a constant vehicle speed without holding his or her foot on the accelerator pedal, and it is operative when the vehicle speed is 25 mph or more."

Americans! How wonderful they were! The cars drove themselves! You pressed Cruise and simply let the car take care of the rest! Marvelous! Rahmid wondered why Epps had not informed him of this feature, and, bitterly, he concluded that Epps was just jealous and wanted to make him work harder. Well, Epps was foiled now. Quickly, Rahmid pulled back on the highway, cutting off several cars in his haste. In moments, he had reached 25 miles per hour, but Rahmid thought he would be extra careful, so he got up to 35 miles per hour before he pressed the Cruise button. There it was. He took his foot off the accelerator, and was proud to see that the Open Road Spectacular kept moving smoothly forward. Rahmid smiled and stretched. It was naptime. Carefully, so as not to disturb the functioning of the machine, Rahmid got up and went to the back of the camper and climbed into his comfortable bed. The Open Road Spectacular drove on, straight ahead, into the sparkling ocean.

Hot
Potato

Doctor Arnold Foretaster was the hottest thing in the Cumberland Gap Memorial Hospital Emergency Room. When he strode through the halls of the hospital with his stethoscope bouncing against his chest, nurses and even doctors stood aside, and tales of his prowess wafted in his wake. He was superhuman. He was amazing. The man had never made a mistake. He had never botched a tracheotomy, never misread the EKG, never diagnosed drug overdose when it was really a psychotic episode. Unerringly, he plucked bullets from vital organs, made dire incisions, and raced alongside gurneys delivering babies. He sewed up adorable children so that they were adorable once more, reattached limbs and digits, and shocked hearts into working again. True, some of his patients died, but that was to be expected in an emergency room and in no way reflected on his skills. There is really nothing for some patients to do but die, and Dr. Foretaster was even renowned for his ability to separate the doomed from the possible survivors in cases of large-scale disaster, such as floods, of which there were many because the Cumberland Gap Memorial Hospital was perched on a particularly unstable bank of the Clinch River just south of the Tennessee border.

Dr. Foretaster's astonishing medical acumen was accompanied by the failing of pride. How could he help it? Even when he was a resident, experienced doctors deferred to his genius. He was the best, not just at Cumberland Gap Memorial, but possibly in the whole state of Tennessee and maybe even the whole country. Not to mention that he was square-jawed and dimple-chinned. Furthermore, his golf game was consistently below par. Sometimes he just couldn't get over himself.

One hot, sticky day in July, Dr. Foretaster was presiding over the emergency room. It was a Saturday, and generally people save their emergencies for Saturday nights, so the afternoon had been fairly slow. A burn victim (trying to burn his car to collect the insurance); a heart attack; another heart attack that Dr. Foretaster immediately diagnosed as heartburn; a broken leg and dislocated elbow; a kid who had swallowed carpet cleaner; and a knife wound. Then, around 2 p.m., an elderly woman came reeling in. Dr. Foretaster, who happened to be standing at the nurse's station, watched her stagger toward the front desk, her face flushed and her dress askew. She almost made it, but with about three feet to go, she crashed to the linoleum.

By the time Dr. Foretaster and Margie, the nurse, reached the other side of the counter, the woman had revived enough to begin moaning. "The vines, the vines," she cried in a dreary wail.

"What?" said Dr. Foretaster and Margie.

But the woman commenced rolling. Up and down the floor she rolled, flinging her arms and legs about in an awkward X as she repeated, "The vines, the viiiiines," in the same moan.

"Cut it out! Get up!" yelled Margie, looming over her.

"The viiiiines!" The woman paid her no mind.

"Hallucinations," said Dr. Foretaster.

"Febrile delusions," said Margie.

Dr. Foretaster looked reflectively at the rolling woman. Restraint seemed to be in order. Now she was bumping into the chairs. "Possible adverse reaction to medication. Possible overdose of hallucinogenic drug."

"At her age?" asked Margie.

"Possible. Possible episode of senile dementia."

"Except it looks like she has a fever."

"The viiiiiiiiiiiines. I got 'em!"

"True. Let's get some restraint going here. Call Ralph."

A few minutes later, Ralph and Margie approached the flailing woman with a gurney featuring a variety of straps. Ralph went down first, with a kick to the testicles. Margie took a punch to the side of the head and spun across the floor herself. Dr. Foretaster realized with disgust that he would have to touch the patient. Quickly he got the old lady in a full Nelson and called for help.

"The vines'll kill me!" she wailed.

Perhaps she was saying "veins," thought Dr. Foretaster. Possible reference to heroin? He looked for tracks, but the old lady's arms were wrinkled and freckled, not to mention moving, and he couldn't really see a thing. Besides, she smelled bad, and he didn't really want to be spending a lot of time with his face in her skin. Nonetheless, he was fairly sure that he was dealing with a psychotropic overdose here, which would explain the fever. It seemed inconsistent with her age and housedress, but, he reminded himself, drug addiction knows no demographic. Besides, addiction causes premature aging. Phew! She really did stink. Like old vegetables.

"I got the vines!" she yowled as the second orderly and Dr. Foretaster heaved her unceremoniously onto the waiting gurney.

Margie was reviving in a corner. "Ugh," she said. "What happened?"

"You got punched," said Dr. Foretaster unsympathetically. "Come here and help me with her. I'm diagnosing psychotropic overdose, so we need to get a urine toxicology screen. But I want a milligram of Ativan first. She's out of control."

"You said it," agreed Margie groggily. "You sure she's overdosing?"

Never before had anyone questioned one of Dr. Foretaster's diagnoses, and he could feel himself recoiling from the shock. "Have I ever been wrong?" he inquired acidly.

"Uh," said Margie, remembering his stature, "no."

"Okay then."

"Vines, vines," cried the woman.

In a matter of minutes, the nameless patient was comfortably lodged on a bed with four-point restraints and the sedative dripping gently into her veins as she murmured about the vines.

Margie was preparing the urine screen. She laid out the catheter and appendant tubes.

"Magazine?" It was Rosa Lee, the world's oldest candy striper. She drove all the nurses crazy because she couldn't see more than two feet ahead of her, so she was always wandering into the emergency ward offering magazines to the nearly dead.

"No, thanks, Rosa Lee," said Margie crisply.

"Help, I got the vines," moaned the patient.

"Ewww, the vines," said Rosa Lee, "That'll put you in the hospital, won't it, darling? Don't worry, though, cause these people here will fix you right smack up."

"What are you talking about?" said Margie quickly.

"The vines, honey," said Rosa Lee. "I know ladies who had 'em, too. You got to pick a fallow potato."

"I got 'em," said the patient proudly.

"What?" asked Margie impatiently, yanking up the patient's dress.

"The vines," said the old woman.

"Stop saying that!" snapped Margie, cutting off her underwear with a pair of large scissors. "Aaaaaaah!" she screamed, as the cloth fell away.

"Yup, you got the vines somethin' fierce," said Rosa Lee.

"What? What?" Dr. Foretaster skidded into the room, but Margie could only point. Curling out of the old woman's private parts were smooth white vines about four inches long. "What the hell is that?" he whispered.

"The vines," explained Rosa Lee.

"The vines," explained the old woman.

"It's a potato," added Rosa Lee helpfully.

"Why? How?" asked Dr. Foretaster weakly.

"To hold it up," said the old woman.

"What up?" he said.

"Her womb, doctor. She put a potato in to hold up her womb, so it wouldn't fall out," said Rosa Lee. Margie gasped.

"'Cause I had so many babies," said the woman.

"How many, darling?" asked Rosa Lee sympathetically.

"Fourteen."

"Well, and no wonder. But you got to pick a fallow potato, else they sprout. See?"

"Couldn't find a fallow one."

"Well, you got to."

"And now I got the vines."

"You got to get it out."

"But I cain't get it out."

They both turned expectantly to Dr. Foretaster.

"He'll get it out, honey. He's a real famous doctor," said Rosa Lee soothingly.

Assuming a look of professional dignity, Dr. Foretaster strode from the room without a word. Hastily, he moved down the hall. He almost made it to the staff restroom before he threw up.